Bygone
HYTHE
with Saltwood, Seabrook and Lympne

A view of Hythe from Mount Street, *c.*1925.

Bygone HYTHE

with Saltwood, Seabrook and Lympne

Charles E. Whitney

Phillimore

1989

Published by
PHILLIMORE & CO. LTD.
Shopwyke Hall, Chichester, Sussex

© Charles E. Whitney, 1989

ISBN 0 85033 675 9

Printed and bound in Great Britain by
BIDDLES LTD.
Guildford, Surrey

For
The Clergy and Congregations
of
The Parish of St Leonard's
Hythe

List of Illustrations

Frontispiece: A view of Hythe from Mount Street, c.1925

1. A drawing of Lympne Castle by George Shepherd, c.1830
2. Saltwood Castle about 1790
3. A map showing the town of Hythe in 1684
4. A print of Hythe drawn by George Shepherd, c.1830
5. Lionel Lukin, lifeboat inventor
6. The first National School in Hythe, 1814
7. Hasted's map of the 'Liberty of Hith', 1799

Lympne

8. Lympne, c.1906
9. A rare photograph showing the forge and stores, c.1906
10. Lympne High Street just after the First World War
11. The interior of Lympne parish church in about 1920
12. Dedication of the Shepway cross in 1923
13. Cinque Ports Flying club, Lympne Airport, c.1934
14. Port Lympne and its gardens

Saltwood

15. Saltwood Castle before its restoration in 1882
16. The gatehouse of Saltwood Castle, c.1880
17. A rare view of Saltwood village green, c.1892
18. Another adjacent view of Saltwood green, c.1892
19. Saltwood green, c.1910
20. The *Castle Hotel*, c.1909
21. Saltwood church, c.1910
22. Interior of Saltwood church early this century
23. W. Clarke's Saltwood Stores' van
24. The Post Office and Schools, Saltwood, c.1905
25. J. E. Wood carriage proprietor, No. 2 Castle Villas
26. Saltwood Cricket Club in the 1940s
27. Alexander Schab operates the Saltwood model railway c.1939

Sandling

28. The old building, Sandling Park
29. Ashford Lodge, Pedlindge, c.1907
30. Workmen who built huts for Kitchener's Army, Sandling, October 1914
31. Pedlindge mission church, early this century
32. Sandling Station, just before the First World War
33. The London train at Sandling Junction, in the 1920s

Seabrook

34. The *Plassey* washed up at Seabrook in January 1883
35. Horn Street, c.1910
36. Horn Street. c.1920
37. The old Horn Street mill of W. Martin Ltd., 1936
38. Carts and waggons outside stables near Mill House, c.1900
39. The old Seabrook lifeboat station
40. A view of Seabrook, c.1900
41. View from Shorncliffe across Seabrook before 1920
42. The main road from Hythe into Seabrook, c.1910
43. *Sea View Hotel*, Seabrook, in 1906
44. The *Fountain Hotel* in 1915
45. Seabrook Church of England School, c.1905
46. A class at Seabrook Church of England School, 1931
47. The funeral of a former police sergeant, Fred Butler, in June 1924
48. 'The Wishing Cap', a children's operetta, performed in 1923
49. Army biplane 269, which crash-landed in Seabrook in 1913

West Hythe

50. Studfall Farm, West Hythe
51. The *Carpenter's Arms*, West Hythe, c.1905
52. Beating the Bounds at West Hythe, 5 October 1910

Hythe

53. A pre-1860 photograph of Hythe
54. General view of Hythe, looking west, early this century
55. View of Hythe at the beginning of this century

Central Hythe

56. High Street, 1872
57. The east end of the High Street at the end of the 19th century
58. The 'Smugglers' Retreat', 1892
59. Hythe High Street in 1899, looking east
60. The west end of the High Street, including the Malthouse

61. Wilberforce Temperance Hotel and Picture Palace
62. No. 18 High Street, 1908
63. Fullager's fishmonger's and poulterer's
64. 'Jumbo' Capon outside his bicycle shop
65. The Old Mill, Mill Lane, c.1908
66. Mackeson's Hythe Brewery in 1909
67. The bottling plant in Mackeson's Brewery, 1909
68. The Metropole Laundry, c.1904
69. Mount Street, c.1925
70. Waggons belonging to Cloake Bros.
71. G. Swain's Albion Garage
72. Edward Uden, baker, grocer and confectioner, Market Street, c.1906
73. Red Lion Square, before the First World War
74. Red Lion Square, photographed between the wars
75. Troops entering Red Lion Square in 1915

Sacred and Secular Buildings
76. The interior of St Leonard's parish church, c.1850
77. Collection of skulls and bones in the parish church
78. The Roman Catholic church, Hythe, 1893
79. The high altar of the Roman Catholic church, c.1900
80. The original Wesleyan Methodist chapel, 1874
81. St Michael's mission church, 1893
82. The Congregational church, High Street
83. The parish church from the south
84. Hythe Institute, Prospect Road
85. Mr. and Mrs. T. Elliott, proprietors of *The Swan*, 1905
86. The 'toast-rack' passing the *Hotel Imperial*, c.1920

Ladies Walk and the Royal Military Canal
87. Ladies Walk in 1870
88. Ladies Walk when flooded by the sea in 1877
89. The original Ladies Walk Bridge
90. The second Ladies Walk Bridge, erected after the 1877 storm
91. Workmen preparing timber for the new Ladies Walk Bridge, c.1877
92. The Royal Military Canal at the beginning of the century
93. C. Carter's boats for hire on the Royal Military Canal

By the Sea
94. No. 5 car of the Hythe and Sandgate Tramway, South Street
95. The Promenade at Hythe, c.1900
96. View along the promenade at the end of the last century
97. Oriental 'new' shelters built before the First World War
98. Hythe coastguards at the end of the last century
99. Results of the storm of 22 March 1913
100. The *Three Brothers* unloading coal, c.1900
101. Seine fishing for mackerel at Hythe
102. Fishermen shaking out herrings on Hythe beach, c.1912
103. Crew of lifeboat No.35 *Meyer de Rothschild*, 1891
104. Old Seabrook lifeboat station, c.1900
105. Toby Griggs and his four sons, 1928
106. Hythe's lifeboat No. 35 *Meyer de Rothschild*, 1907
107. The original lifeboat house in 1934

Railways
108. H.R.H. the Duke of York, driving the the *Green Goddess* on 5 August 1926
109. Mr. Hardy, first Stationmaster of Hythe Station
110. Hythe Station and railway staff, c.1904
111. Bobby Burn with a Southern Railway delivery waggon

Glimpses of Bygone Hythe
112. Lower and Stade Windmills, pre-1877
113. A Hythe windmill, Ruckinge
114. Looking north towards Cold Harbour Farm
115. Stade Street and South Road, Hythe
116. Hythe Theatre poster
117. Programme for a musical and theatrical entertainment at the Hythe Institute, August 1896
118. *Hotel Imperial*, c.1919
119. The station omnibus in Douglas Avenue in the 1930s
120. Houses in South Road and Parade in January 1877 when the sea flooded the area
121. Hythe Fire Brigade outside the engine house, c.1900
122. The 'christening' of the new fire engine, April 1905
123. Burch's carnival waggon
124. Hythe Town Military Band, 1893
125. Hythe Town Excelsior Band on Hythe green, c.1900
126. Hythe National Reserve Band, 1913
127. The proclamation of King George V at Hythe Town Hall, 14 May 1910
128. 'Titanic Sunday' parade, 28 April 1912
129. Hythe's G.P.O. staff in 1912
130. The Brotherhood and Guestling of the Cinque Ports leaving the parish church, June 1910
131. Brotherhood and Guestling procession
132. The Brotherhood and Guestling outside the *Hotel Imperial*
133. Richard O'Gorman in the uniform of the Kent Volunteer Fencibles
134. The Rev. Richard O'Gorman O.S.A.
135. Paddock House Hospital, June 1917
136. Sir Edward Sassoon, Hythe's M.P. from 1889 to 1912
137. Election campaigners in Mackeson's brewery yard
138. Sir Philip Sassoon M.P., July 1919
139. Hythe War Memorial in the 1920s
140. Hythe Venetian Fête in 1938

The School of Musketry
141. The School of Musketry at Hythe in 1860
142. Rifle practice ground of the School of Musketry
143. A first class certificate in Musketry presented in 1874
144. Regiments represented at the School of Musketry march to Hythe parish church
145. Officers' Mess, School of Musketry, c.1905
146. Lecture room at the School of Musketry, c.1905
147. Rifle instruction class on Hythe green, c.1900
148. The cracked Martello tower in 1913
149. Small Arms School shooting team, 1934

Education and Recreation
150. Hythe National Schools, St Leonard's Place, c.1880
151. A class from Hythe Junior School, c.1914
152. Hythe Girls' School, Class I, 1914
153. Hythe Girls' School (St Leonard's), Class I, c.1928
154. Patrol leader C. Capon of the 1st Hythe B.P. Scout Troop
155. Cecil Oliver, one of the 'Coastwatching Scouts', 1914
156. Sir Robert Baden-Powell visiting a Hythe scout leaders' course in 1913
157. The entire Hythe Scout Troop, 1909
158. Bowling match, Boxing Day 1905
159. Mr. Ray Munds, groundsman at the cricket and bowls clubs
160. Winners of the 50 guinea Hythe Challenge Cup, 1910
161. A pre-First World War tennis tournament at the *Hotel Imperial*
162. Hythe Football Club's team for the 1910-11 season
163. Sunday League footballers from the 1910-11 season
164. Hythe C.C. v M.C.C., Cricket Week in August 1905
165. A. P. F. (Percy) Chapman, captain of Hythe, Kent and England

The End of an Era
166. Bomb damage in the High Street, 4 October 1940
167. Initial clearance of High Street bomb damage
168. Bomb damage close to St Leonard's parish church, 1940

The author would like to acknowledge the use of the photographs and ephemera in this book as follows: Mrs. Molly Griggs for nos. 3 (with the additional permission of the Trustees of the Hospitals of St Bartholomew and St John), 59, 80, 96, 100, 101, 102, 103, 105, 107, 113, 114, 125, 128; Mr. Frank Martin for no. 5; Miss Flora Laundon for no. 6; Mrs. Sheila Mallinder for nos. 8-11, 13, 24-33, 115; Mr. John Rendle for nos. 12, 20, 42, 50, 60, 68, 72, 79, 85, 86, 92, 94, 108 (with the additional permission of Romney, Hythe and Dymchurch Light Railway), 129, 134, 135, 144, 146, 149, 160, 161; Mr. Jerry Blanchet for nos. 14, 93, 99, 122, 126; Mr. Eamonn Rooney for nos. 15-19, 21-23, 51, 56, 58, 65, 75, 78, 84, 90, 106, 112 (with the late Mr. C. P. Davies), 117, 130, 132, 137, 139, 150; Mrs. Anne Bamford for nos. 34, 35, 37 (with the late Mr. C. P. Davies), 38 (with Mrs. M. B. Hazard), 39-41, 43-49; Mr. Bernard Mundel for nos. 36, 57, 61, 63, 69, 71, 73, 74, 82, 87-89, 95, 97, 98, 104, 121, 127, 133, 136, 138, 145, 147, 153; Mr. Charles Swan for nos. 52, 64, 70, 109 (with the additional permission of Romney, Hythe and Dymchurch Light Railway), 118, 123, 131, 140, 151, 152, 158, 159, 162, 163, 166-168 (the last three with the additional permission of Mr. Brian Lewis, Editor, *Kentish Express*; Miss Muriel Sharp for nos. 53 (with Mrs. Evelyn Dray), 91, 110; Mr. David Cole for nos. 54, 83; Mr. Nicholas Redman and the Whitbread Archive Collection for nos. 66, 67; The Rev. Norman Woods, Vicar of Hythe, for nos. 76, 81; Mr. Sidney Burn for no. 111; Mr. Peter Bamford for nos. 120, 143, 148; Mr. Keith Archer and the Hythe Town Military Band for no. 124; Major 'Dougie' Maber M.B.E. for nos. 141, 142; Mr. John Schoner and 1st Hythe Scouts for nos. 154-157; Richard Hook M.B.E. and Hythe Cricket Club for nos. 164, 165. Nos. 1, 2, 4, 7, 55, 77 came from the author's own collection. The cover photograph was taken by Mr. John Davies.

Acknowledgements

This volume would not have been completed without the enthusiastic support of many people, including a number of major collectors of photographs in the area. On Hythe itself I am particularly grateful for the generosity of Molly Griggs, Bernard Mundel, John Rendle, Eamonn Rooney, Muriel Sharp and Charles Swan. Seabrook and the surrounding locality was largely covered by Anne Bamford's excellent collection, while on Saltwood and Lympne Sheila Mallinder's collection was outstanding. A number of other equally kind people contributed valuable photographs and ephemera, and I should like to thank Peter Bamford, Jerry Blanchet, Sidney Burn, David Cole, Evelyn Dray, Mrs. M. B. Hazard, Flora Laundon, Maurice Newman, Major 'Dougie' Maber M.B.E. and Gerald Walter.

Among organisations who have helped, lent items or given permission for reproduction I would like to thank Frank Martin of the Hythe Branch of the R.N.L.I.; John Schoner, Group Scout Leader, 1st Hythe Scouts; Keith Archer of Hythe Town Military Band; the Rev. Norman Woods, vicar of Hythe; Don Symonds, Jean Zabell, Honorary Secretary, and Richard Hook M.B.E., President of Hythe Cricket Club; Nicholas Redman and the Whitbread Archive Collection; Brian Lewis, editor of the *Kentish Express*; the Trustees of St Bartholomew's and St John's Hospitals, Hythe, and their Clerk, Tim Lawrence; the Romney, Hythe and Dymchurch Light Railway; Major M. Fogwell (Retired), Museum Curator and Corps Adjutant, School of Infantry, Warminster. Major 'Dougie' Maber M.B.E. (Retired), Former Range Commandant at Hythe, and President of Hythe Bowls Club, took a close personal interest and was particularly supportive. My thanks to Alan Taylor must be coupled with Folkestone and District Local History Society, of which he is Honorary Secretary. Several members helped to fill perplexing gaps in information. I am also grateful to Alan for making available research notes made by the late C. P. Davies, a noted local historian.

A number of people assisted me with information, books or both, and I should like to thank Bruce Davis, Norah Osborne, Barbara Mountjoy, Captain Slade (Salvation Army), the late Jack Goddard, and Tony and Anne Marston. Muriel Sharp and Jack Barker, Honorary Archivist, St Leonard's Church, Hythe, have both spent years delving into different aspects of Hythe's history: their kindness and deep knowledge were invaluable.

I am grateful to the staff at Folkestone Reference Library and particularly Kit Cooney and Mary Duncombe at Hythe Library for their patient help. The research work done by Pat Miller, Jan Nicholls and Kay Allen was also much appreciated. Thanks, too, must go to John Davies for his excellent cover photograph.

Nick Brodrick, headmaster of Dover College Junior School, Folkestone, generously allowed me to use facilities at the school.

Jack Barker, Mary Duncombe, Molly and Sonny Griggs and Eamonn Rooney kindly gave the draft text their critical attention and made valuable suggestions.

My daughters, Heather and Louise, put up with a preoccupied father with remarkably good grace. Anne, my wife, was as supportive as ever; without her considerable assistance the book would not have been completed on time.

Frances Mee of Phillimore produced order out of potential chaos with her customary efficiency and charm.

Trouble has been taken to seek all necessary permissions and to eliminate errors. Should there be anything amiss, I apologise.

Introduction

'Hythe' is derived from an Old English word meaning a landing place, a haven. It has been spelt in a variety of ways such as 'Hethe' and 'Hithe'.

The key to the development of Hythe lies in the geography of the northern edge of Romney Marsh and the tactical decisions of the Romans when they finally mounted a full-scale invasion in A.D. 43. There was some Roman occupation of Hythe: finds at Harpswood and at the corner of North Road and Tanner's Hill confirm this. However, the Romans in general were more attracted to the tidal estuary of the River Limen just to the south. On the north bank they built a fort, later called Studfall Castle. The harbour became *Portus Lemanis*, and was connected by Stone Street to Canterbury and from there to London. *Portus Lemanis* was one of three major entrances to England, the others being Dover and Richborough. Archaeologists have concluded from coins found on site that Roman occupation of the fort lasted from about A.D. 250 to no later than A.D. 350. Then, international pressures led the troops to move to the continent, while geographic changes may have already resulted in the partial silting up of the estuary. At one stage the fort was part of the national defences under the overall control of the Count of the Saxon Shore. Excavations between 1978-81 have indicated that there was a shore base of the Roman fleet in Britain, the *Classis Britannica*, between the Roman fort and West Hythe. Built long before the fort, its exact site is unknown.

The gradual silting up of the northern end of Romney Marsh probably encouraged a movement of population north-eastwards along the coast, first to West Hythe, and then to Hythe itself. By late Saxon times the small cluster of dwellings which had guarded a lagoon or haven, probably to service the manor of Saltwood, had grown to a sizeable community. The port of Hythe was established. The inlet which helped to create it was described by H. D. Dale in his *The Ancient Town of Hythe and St Leonard's Church, Kent* thus:

> ... an inlet of the sea came in between the Stade [the stand or landing place] and Twiss Road. The water flowed over the present cricket and recreation grounds, and then, taking a westerly direction, went in as far as West Hythe, forming a lagoon which was sheltered from the open sea by the great bank of shingle which still exists, stretching from Hythe along the Dymchurch Road.

There was an eastern 'arm' to the lagoon, too, stretching down towards Seabrook.

Hythe was used as a port for more than just military and fishing purposes. It probably exported wool and cheese, both highly prized on the continent, as well as being a general point of embarkation, especially for France.

The first document indisputably associated with Hythe – or 'Hethe' as it was then – dates from 1036. In this, Halden (or Halfden), a thane, gave the manor of Saltwood which included Hythe to Christchurch, Canterbury. It was transferred a short time later to the Archbishop of Canterbury who administered it through the judicious use of a bailiff for the next 500 years.

In Hythe little pre-Conquest building has survived except for a few stones of St Leonard's church, which J. F. Barker has recently confirmed are Saxon in origin. He has also forcefully argued that the 'round' tower in the body of the parish church may well be a former Saxon watchtower, too. Another trace of early Hythe would be the trackway, now Church Hill, which probably led from the Stade to the castle at Saltwood. John Guy in *Kent Castles* declares that Saltwood Castle was originally a fortress built by Aesc in 488. There may even have been a watchtower there. An old Roman track overlooking the coastline as it was then would also have existed – the present North Road.

In the late 10th or early 11th century ships from five south-eastern ports – Sandwich, Dover, Hythe, Romney and Hastings – met off East Anglia in order to land herrings at what is now Great Yarmouth. There was a loose affiliation. King Edward the Confessor had an arrangement with some, though probably not all, of them to supply ships and men but this system was not to evolve further for some years. However, that did not save Hythe in 1052, according to Sir Charles Igglesden, when Earl Godwin, Earl of Wessex which by then included Kent, was banished from England by Edward together with Godwin's sons. They collected a fleet of ships and attacked the Kent coast. At Hythe, Igglesden believes, 'They destroyed all the ships that lay in the harbour, and the inhabitants were put to the sword by the hundred'. In the end, Godwin forced Edward to take him back.

William I instigated the Domesday Survey in 1085-6. The manor of Saltwood is recorded as having 47 villagers, smallholders and slaves plus wives and children. Hythe consisted of 225 burgesses plus another six who had somehow found themselves in Lyminge calculations, together with their families. Interestingly, although a church in Saltwood manor is recorded, there is no specific mention of Hythe churches. However, two churches are mentioned in *Domesday Monachorum* as being in Hythe. St Leonard's and St Mary's West Hythe are identified on this list as paying dues to Christ's Church Canterbury by 1070.

Lympne was by now comparatively small, with one villager who rated slightly above a smallholder, 18 smallholders, their families and some seven priests, presumably serving in some sort of community. At this time Lympne seems to have belonged to Aldington manor. The new Norman Archbishop of Canterbury, Lanfranc, built the church at Lympne and also decreed that it and the fortified residence built at the same time, Lympne Castle, should belong to the Archdeacon of Canterbury.

There are few glimpses of 12th-century life in Hythe. A silver penny dating from the middle of that century was found with nearly 200 others near Linton, Maidstone, in 1883. George Wakeford identified it as belonging to a Hythe mint, the mintmaster apparently named Estmund. The identification must be treated with care: if true, it underlines Hythe's importance as a centre of medieval trade.

It was to Hythe that four knights – William de Tracey, Reginald Fitzures, Hugh de Morville and Richard le Breton – sailed from Normandy in December 1170, having heard King Henry II's denunciation of Archbishop Thomas Becket, according to H. F. Abell in his *History of Kent*. Hythe was one of four principal ports of Kent at this time, the others being Sandwich, Dover and Romney. The knights are said to have been met at Saltwood Castle by the unsavoury Sir Ranulf de Broc, a local man who had been appointed castellan by Henry II so that Becket could not attempt repossession. It was there that the murder of Becket was apparently plotted, de Broc sending his son Robert and an escort of cavalry with the murderers down Stone Street to Canterbury. Becket was butchered in his cathedral on 29 December. The knights are believed to have returned to Saltwood to confer with Sir Ranulf before going their separate ways. Sir Ranulf added a tower keep at about this time to the original castle whose main curtain walls had been built some years earlier by Henry I's standard bearer, Henry de Essex. With de Broc's tower keep in place, the castle was little changed over the next two centuries until the time of Archbishop

1. Lympne Castle with Lympne church to the right and behind it, drawn by George Shepherd in about 1830 and engraved by H. Adland.

2. Saltwood Castle about 1790. The earthquake in 1580 rendered it uninhabitable for hundreds of years and there was some pilfering of the fabric for building materials. Restoration began in earnest towards the end of the 19th century and continued into the twentieth.

Courtenay in the late 14th century. The earliest part of the present Saltwood church dates from *c.*1150, the tower with its original gabled top dating from *c.*1200.

In the 13th century the Cinque Port fleet, to which Hythe contributed, had been in action. In 1217, 40 Cinque Port boats under Hubert de Burgh faced 80 sail bringing reinforcements to Prince Louis of France, who was attempting to capture the English throne. By the judicious use of prevailing winds and quick-lime, the English won. In 1277 a Cinque Port fleet helped Edward I to defeat the Welsh Prince Llewelyn ap Gruffydd by cutting him off from his supply base at Anglesey. Igglesden mentions an attack on Hythe in 1295 (Hasted says 1293) by Frenchmen sailing galleys. The attack failed: over 240 raiders were reported killed. In 1300 according to Dale (Forbes says 1335), 'Hythe furnished only three ships for the King's service'. Yet Henry III's instructions issued in 1229 had said Hythe was to provide five ships, fully crewed. Certainly, Hythe fishermen were always ready to fight. In 1302 when the Cinque Ports and Yarmouth ships were lying in a harbour in Flanders a fight broke out among them, the crew of one Hythe boat inflicting considerable damage on their opponents. Edward I held a judicial inquiry into the incident and the Hythe men were duly censured.

By 1345, Hythe was fully discharging her obligations regarding ship service, sending six ships to the siege of Calais at the request of Edward III, who had earlier threatened to cancel Hythe's privileges if the ships were not provided. It was perhaps during this period that Hythe reached the height of its success as a medieval port. The parish church had already been enlarged and the magnificent chancel begun. Bishop Hamo of Rochester, a native of Hythe, was extending his family home in order that it might accommodate 10, later 13, needy men and women. The site was to become St Bartholomew's Hospital. The house, 'Centuries', is no longer a hospital or almshouse but is still in St Bartholomew's Street. A forerunner may have been in Saltwood. The hospital began its work in 1336, according to Professor W. K. Jordan. St John's Hospital in the High Street was founded at about the same time. In Edward VI's reign (1547-53) the administration of St John's was overhauled and it became an almshouse. Forbes notes that St Bartholomew's was certainly in continuous use from 1819 and that it was after the excavations of the Second World War that the inmates were transferred to St John's.

The 14th century had seen Hythe rise to its zenith as a port; its success was not to last. The Brodhull or gathering of the Cinque Ports at Hythe in the middle 1360s probably marks the height of its medieval influence. In 1400 Hythe not only lost five ships and 100 men at sea but the town was ravaged by fire, some 200 dwellings being lost, according to William Lambarde. Henry IV was petitioned to allow the townsfolk to leave Hythe altogether. Henry refused but exempted Hythe from ship service for five years. This exemption was later extended and after 1414 Hythe never again gave ship service in full.

Living in Hythe at this time must have been distinctly unpleasant. The stench was considerable, heaps of dung sometimes blocking progress in parts of the town. In 1473, as Dulley reminds us, one John Edwey left 3s. 4d. 'to making of one common latrine in the town'. However, life then was not entirely depressing. There were weekly markets. Hythe players performed and journeyed to other towns, presenting the Passion and other sacred plays in New Romney and Lydd in 1466. They went to New Romney again in 1482, 1486, 1494 and 1503.

At the beginning of the 16th century, 'Romney, despite the efforts of its burghers, had practically given way as a port to Hythe, and Hythe was already on its downward course' (H. F. Abell). The reasons were shingle and silt. However, trade was beginning to improve and hops had been introduced into Kent from Flanders. Records of a court of inquiry held on the sea shore at Hythe in June 1521 have been unearthed. Sir Edward Poynyngs, Lord Warden of the Cinque Ports, presided. Matthew Lewes was 'presented' for fishing with his nets before sunrise about the feast of Pentecost. As this was breaking the law, Matthew was fined. At the same inquiry, a Hythe servant, William Andrew, and a butcher from Lydd, Strogell, were fined for taking a salmon out of the net of John Sutton of Folkestone.

During the reign of Henry VIII (1509-47), international tension gradually rose. In 1522, the Archbishop of Canterbury, William Wareham, is said to have personally inspected Folkestone, Sandwich, Dover, Deal and Hythe, '... that he might cause efficient means to be taken for the defence of these towns'. He wrote to the King's chief minister, Cardinal Wolsey, on 31 October 1522 '... assuring him that watches and beacons should be set up all along the coast ...'. Tension rose further and the order for Sandgate Castle to be constructed was made in 1539. W. L. Rutton has researched the contribution Hythe made. 'Michael Carver was paid 5s. for stone delivered to the Castle', he notes, while of the 147,000 bricks used, 'Hythe ... produced small quantities'. Coal '... was brought to Hythe in two ships ... the total quantities unshipped at Hythe and thence brought by boats to Sandgate was 96 Chaldrons', which is about 23 cwt., at 6s. 8d. per chaldron. Poles for scaffolding came from 'Sandlygs' (Sandling?) and 'Brock Hill'. Four thousand 'Sprygg' nails were bought at Hythe for 2s. 8d.

Meanwhile, Thomas Cromwell, now the King's chief minister, had become Earl of Essex in 1540, acquiring lands which included the manor of Saltwood and its castle. Later the same year he was arrested on a trumped up charge of treason and executed. It was also about this time that the room known as the parvise above the south porch in the parish church was first used as a town hall. This continued until the corporation moved to the present town hall in 1794.

The Marian persecution of Protestants resulted in four victims from Hythe. Robert Streater and George Catmer were burnt at the stake in Canterbury in 1555, George's widow Joan in 1556 and William Hay in 1557. There were imprisonments for heresy, too.

In 1575, Queen Elizabeth I granted Hythe a Charter, by which it ceased to be subservient to the Archbishop of Canterbury and became master of its own affairs with its own Mayor and Corporation. The Archbishop's last bailiff, John Bridgeman, became Hythe's first Mayor, a fact recorded on a plaque in the parish church.

The 1580 earthquake destroyed part of Saltwood Castle, making it unsuitable as a defence point a few years later when the Spanish Armada threatened. The earthquake made the Hythe bells ring, probably weakening the tower; it may also have caused the collapse of a hostelry on the site of the *White Hart*.

Hythe felt the last of Elizabeth's tongue when it was accused, with other Cinque Ports, of harbouring pirates and receiving pirated goods.

Although the harbour had virtually silted up by now, according to the Customs Port Books of 1565, Hythe was still enjoying a thriving trade in exporting horses.

Hythe was required to produce a pinnace as its contribution to defence against the Spanish Armada in 1588. This was the 50-ton *Grace of God* commanded by Captain William Fordred, a Hythe name that has survived into this present century. Forbes considers it possible that, as in the case of New Romney and Lydd, the boat was hired. Abell and others assert that the Cinque Ports held in readiness many smaller vessels – probably lightly-armed fishing boats with crews of up to six men. Hythe is said to have prepared twelve. Other defences were prepared too. Perhaps this was the occasion when a battery was first mounted at the end of Mount Street on a site where the Hythe Institute used to be. The official victory service for the defeat of the Armada, held in St Paul's Cathedral in London on Sunday 24 November 1588, was conducted by the Dean, Dr. Alexander Nowell, who had been Rector of Saltwood with Hythe in 1559-60.

Though its importance as a port had diminished, Hythe continued as a fishing centre of some size. In 1566, according to Dulley's work, '... there were 122 houses in the town and 160 occupants engaged in fishing'. He also notes that the smaller boats at Hythe '... were sometimes referred to ... as "stade boats", the stade being the open beach where they were hauled up by means of "vernes" or capstans worked by horses. These capstans were a common item in wills.'

The 17th-century political situation was unsettled. The Lord Wardens of the Cinque Ports such as the Duke of Buckingham endeavoured to keep the ports, which were often 'pocket boroughs', under their own influence. Later, William Brockman of Beachborough was one of few Royalists in the area, most people siding with Parliament. On the election of Oliver Cromwell as Lord Protector in 1653, the Mayor and Corporation feasted themselves at what is now the *King's Head*.

The same century saw smuggling, not unknown before, become rife along the coastline from Thanet to Romney Marsh and beyond, not least at Hythe. The reason for this upsurge was, as Abell tells us, that 'In 1630 the King [Charles I] endeavoured to add to his revenue by prohibiting the export of wool, although he sold the privilege. This put a

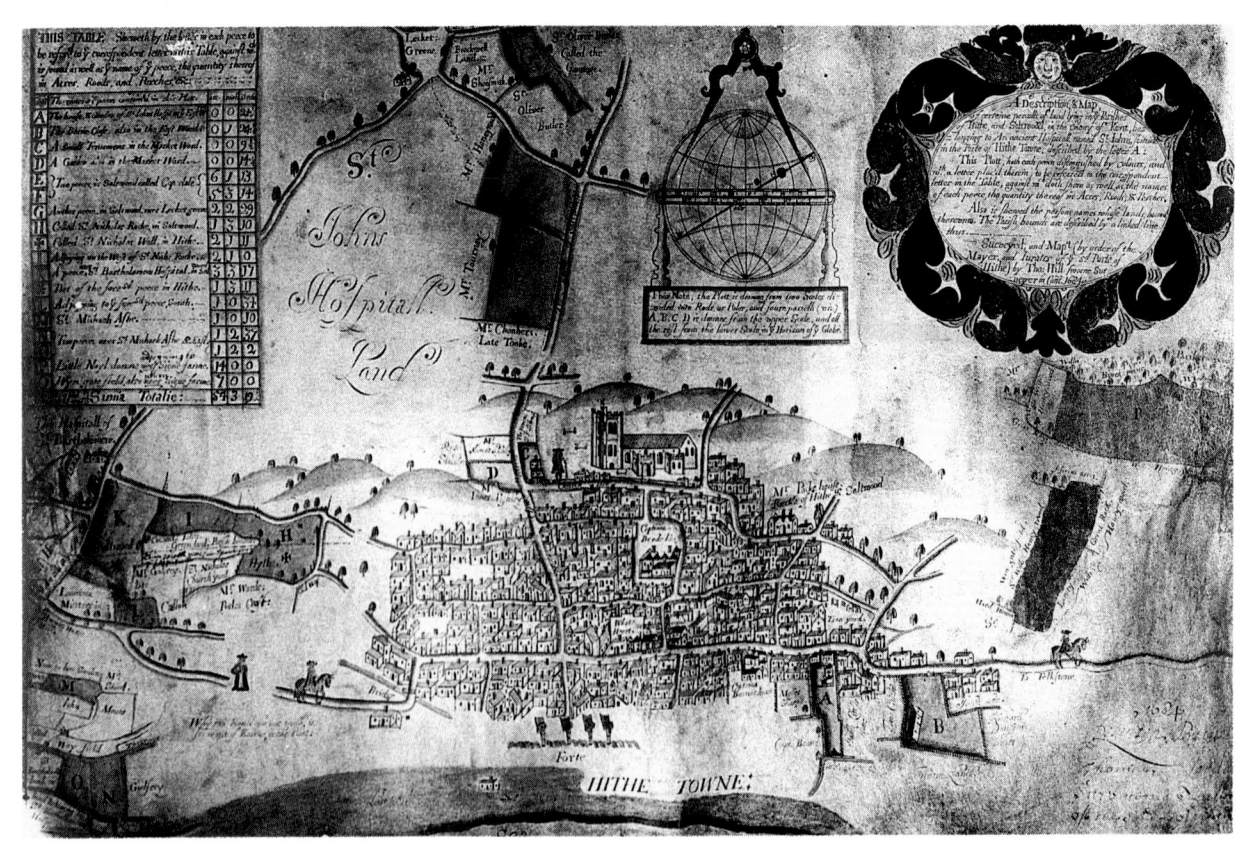

3. A map showing the town of Hythe (Hithe) in 1684. Its main purpose was to indicate the location of property belonging to St John's Hospital.

premium upon smuggling, which was carried out to an enormous extent on the Kentish coast ...'. This wool smuggling was nicknamed 'owling' and it was not only poor fishermen who were involved. In 1692, 16 bags of wool were seized in Scotney barn which belonged to Julius Deedes, then Mayor of Hythe. Fourteen of his men attacked the revenue officers and succeeded in retrieving the wool. At the subsequent trial, Deedes achieved an acquittal. Political skullduggery also continued. At Hurst, on the hills above Lympne, Barclay's or Fenwick's Jacobite plot of 1696 was hatched. The idea was to murder King William III as he went riding in Richmond Park. The plot was betrayed, Fenwick tried to escape to France but was found in bed and was eventually beheaded on Tower Hill.

In 1620, the Church of Our Lady of West Hythe was burnt down and never repaired. Later the same century Professor Burrows notes that in 1674 '... an opening was made "at or neere a place called Shorncliff"', a last attempt to recreate a harbour but this proved as unsuccessful as other efforts over the previous 200 years.

A disaster nearly occurred in the next century when the west tower of St Leonard's collapsed in May 1739. Six people waiting to climb it narrowly escaped with their lives. It was not entirely unexpected as a vestry meeting in 1736 had noted the '... ruinous and dangerous condition' of the tower, almost certainly caused by the earthquake of 1580. Although bell-ringing had been restricted, little else had been done. A new tower was built in 1750, possibly 12 feet lower than the original. Julius Deedes paid for much of the work. This could have influenced the decision to allow his family to rebuild and restore the south transept of the parish church known as St James's chapel, build their family vault underneath and have rights to pews in the transept. Hence from 1751 it has been known as the Deedes chapel.

The 18th century was marked by the irregularities apparent in the election of Hythe M.P.s. For example, in the election of 1710 illegal soliciting of votes, bribery, abuse of the Mayoral office, lack of payment of poor rates and other offences were all prevalent. At local government level one man, Robert Tournay, regularly became Mayor while also being Town Clerk. Eighteenth-century Hythe seems to have been dominated by a clique of families which Forbes identified as the Deedes, Tournays, Brockmans, Botelers and Haleses, some of whom did not live in the town. In 1771 a Masonic lodge was established and the new town hall, with a small jail underneath, was completed in 1794. Hythe had its fishing, smuggling, trading vessels, market days, inns and some shops but it was small and as a centre of trade cannot have been that important. Its population had declined since Tudor times, but the next century witnessed great change.

The end of the 18th century and the beginning of the 19th saw a rather anxious government decide that, in the light of Napoleon's invasion threat, steps would have to be taken to defend the country, especially the vulnerable south-east coast. In 1794, Shorncliffe army camp was opened on 229 acres which the government had bought a year or two earlier. General Sir John Moore, later posthumous hero of the Battle of Corunna, was responsible for the brigade stationed at Shorncliffe in 1803. He had a house in Hythe.

Some say that it was the local top military engineer, Colonel (later Brigadier) Twiss, after whom the fort and road is named, who suggested the idea of Martello towers, based on the sturdy, effective defence tower at Cape Martella, Corsica. Others maintain that the credit for the original idea should go to Captain W. H. Ford, Royal Engineers, who had seen the Corsican tower in action. Construction began in 1805. The cost was higher than the estimated £3,000 each. Every Martello tower required half a million bricks and supported a 24-pound gun mounted on the roof. Quarters for one officer and at least 24 other ranks were provided. The towers, many of which still survive, stretched from

Folkestone round to Seaford in Sussex. In Hythe they ranged from Number 10, which used to stand on the edge of what is now Hythe Imperial golf course, to Number 19, right along the Hythe military ranges. In addition to these towers there were three forts or redoubts. At the end of Twiss Road was Twiss Fort. At the other end of Hythe was Sutherland Fort, while Montcrieff Fort was further along the coast towards Dymchurch.

The second decision regarding the defence of the area was to go ahead with the building of the Royal Military Canal. Captain Wrottesley, Royal Engineers, reporting on the canal in 1857, is very precise regarding its statistics. 'It is nearly 19 miles in length from the sea at Shornliffe to the River Rother, and 7 miles from the latter place to Cliff End near Winchelsea. It was excavated ... twenty yards in breadth, to hold nine feet of water in the middle'. It was agreed between William Pitt, General Moore, Brigadier Twiss and the Romney Marsh Lords of the Level that the Marsh, which was seen as a likely enemy landing place, could be flooded. As Frank Jessup has indicated, the canal had two purposes: 'To enable soldiers and their supplies to be moved from one part of the coast to another ... and to hold up the enemy's advance if he succeeded in making a landing at Romney Marsh.' Movement would be helped by building a military road on the landward side of the canal. About every 40 metres there was to be a 'kink' in the canal where a cannon could be stationed to command the adjacent stretch of water, thereby further impeding the enemy's advance. The consulting engineer, John Rennie, tried to build it with civilian labour and a little military help but in 1805 the task was handed over to the army almost entirely. The project was completed in 1809. Many barracks appeared in Hythe. At the very beginning of the century, they were built on the site of the present

4. This well known print of Hythe was drawn by George Shepherd, engraved by C. Bedford and published in 1829. It shows the extent of the town, the recently completed Royal Military Canal with its military road, and barracks on the left which were later incorporated into the School of Musketry. Two Martello towers and Fort Twiss can be seen close to the sea.

'Seeboard' buildings. The military historian A. J. Parsons believes that they were built primarily for the Royal Staff Corps while the canal was built but, as construction did not begin until 1804, they may have had other functions. There was accommodation for about 300 men including 'comfortable rooms' for married soldiers. Men of the Royal Waggon Train – disbanded in 1833 at Hythe – were housed in temporary barracks on the canal field site which was in the area between Scanlon's Bridge and the Duke's Head Bridge. The main barracks continued to be used by the Royal Staff Corps until peace came again in 1815. The 29th Foot and detachments of other regiments were stationed there, one of their duties being to act as guards for the part of Shorncliffe barracks that had been made 'a place of confinement for lunatics'. The establishment of the military in Hythe was to prove a valued source of income for the town for the next 150 years.

The appearance of so many barracks, including some on Barrack Hill, clearly altered the western approach to the town. William Cobbett in his *Rural Rides* was one who disapproved of the whole military effort when he visited the town in the 1820s and opined 'Hythe is half barracks; the hills are covered in barracks; and barracks most expensive, most squandering, fill up the side of the hill'.

The School of Musketry at Hythe had opened by October 1853. Its first commandant was Lt.-Col. G. Crawford Hay who is said to have fired from Hythe churchyard at a target set up on the beaches a mile away. One wonders how safe the shooting was! Colonel Hay's task was to create a corps of experts on rifle shooting – especially, initially, the Minié rifle and also the Enfield .557 calibre rifle. The corps was to 'develop and improve the imperfect early rifle and disseminate knowledge of rifle shooting throughout the army', as Parsons puts it. In 1919 the School of Musketry became the Small Arms Wing until 1926. It changed its name fairly frequently after that but settled for Small Arms Wing, School of Infantry, in 1950 until it finally closed in Hythe in 1968. In 1953, centenary year, the Mayor and Corporation of Hythe conferred the Freedom of the Borough on the Small Arms Wing. The Hythe ranges themselves are still in use today.

Soldiers coming to Hythe did more than simply provide extra spending power in the neighbourhood. The Rev. Hubert Pitts has concluded that it is probable that 'godly soldiers' were at least in part responsible for bringing Methodism to the town at the very beginning of the 19th century. Barrack Master Duncan McDiarmid may well have been prominent in this connection, although there appear to have been a number of committed civilians, too. In the early summer of 1813 they rented, for £4 per year, a small chapel at the corner of Conduit Street and Bartholomew Street, which had previously been used by local Baptists, who had preceeded the Methodists into Hythe. The original Methodist chapel in Rampart Road was built in 1845. The better-built present chapel was dedicated in 1898 in a decade in which a surprising number of places of worship were opened. The Roman Catholics dedicated their present church in 1893, the same year as St Michael's mission church, a daughter church of St Leonard's, was opened in Portland Road. The Salvation Army, which had an 'outpost' in Hythe under the control of the Folkestone Corps, officially established the Hythe Corps in February 1896. The first officer in charge was a woman, Captain Hands. Originally based in a hall next to the *Hope Inn* stables in Albert Lane, they moved to their present hall in 1910. It should also be said that the parish church itself had been restored, which had included the completion of the chancel during the 1870s and 1880s. A few years earlier, in 1868, the Congregational church was built in the High Street. It was demolished in 1988.

A remarkable divine at this time was the Rev. James Croft (1784-1869). He was rector of Saltwood and, until 1844 when it finally became a separate parish, Hythe. He was also, simultaneously, incumbent of Lympne, West Hythe and nine other parishes, Archdeacon and Canon of Canterbury, earning nearly £5,000 a year in total. He achieved all this by the simple expedient of marrying a daughter of the Archbishop of Canterbury. He gave his Saltwood curate £50 per year.

The military brought with them a desire for more than just spiritual refreshment. William and Henry Mackeson of Deal, who came to appreciate this very early on, bought Hythe brewery from John Friend in October 1801, together with ten 'inns'. Although there is evidence that there had been some brewing in the town since the 15th century, the brewery itself can only be traced back as far as 1669 when it was owned by James Pashley. From the beginning of the 19th century onwards the brewery prospered but it was the introduction of 'Mackeson's Milk Stout' in 1907 that was to lead to Mackeson's becoming nationally known. Eventually the firm was bought by Whitbread's. The last brew in Hythe was on 18 April 1968.

An old public house is the *Bell Inn* which is said to date back well over 400 years. Michael Mirams considers that much of the timber used for its weatherboarding came from wrecks off Romney Marsh, at a time when the *Bell* stood not so far from the water's edge.

The White Hart, too, is an ancient hostelry. Deeds dated 1648 allude to two previous owners, tending to confirm the architectural evidence which indicates a Tudor building. John Kett believes that the original inn was built about 1290 and was destroyed by fire. The subsequent building was also destroyed, this time by the earthquake of 1580. The present hostelry was erected not long after that. Kett considers that the inn's name comes from '... the shape of the headdress worn by lay sisters who had ministered to the pilgrims' who passed through Hythe. Mirams considers that the White Hart, a symbol of King Richard II (1377-99), may well be the real reason for the name. *The Swan Hotel* was first mentioned in the early 16th century. In the 18th century it was seen as one of the top inns in Kent. Tsar Alexander of Russia and the Duchess of Oldenburg took tea there when passing through Hythe in 1814. *The King's Head* adopted that name in 1750. Previously it had been known as the *George* (1584) and the *Sun* (1714). *The Duke's Head* was opened in 1810 and was patronised particularly by the local farming fraternity that came to the market. The present *Red Lion* featured in Russell Thorndike's tales of 'Dr Syn', the fictional smuggler. It was known originally as the *Three Mariners* in 1670.

Smuggling other than 'owling' was escalating, notably in spirits, wine, lace, silk, tea and tobacco. There were many hiding places in Hythe. One was close to the *Bell Inn* where there was a tunnel by an underground millstream. Here, casks of gin and brandy were stored out of harm's way. The authorities tried to take the initiative. By 1800, 13 revenue craft covered the Kent and Sussex coastline. In June 1817 an unsuccessful coast blockade was attempted which continued until 1831. Martello towers were used to garrison troops against smugglers. One of the biggest, most infamous gangs was the Ransley or Aldington band, also sometimes called the 'Blues'. Under their leader, George Ransley, they were active in Romney Marsh and sometimes the area around Hythe. One night in August 1826, at Fort Montcrieff, Lieutenant Johnstone and his patrol came across a large galley which had been beached and was being unloaded. There was a battle; the smugglers retreated into the marsh leaving one wounded man behind. Eventually, many of the gang were caught and transported to Australia, probably only escaping the gallows because of the skill of their lawyer, a Mr. Platt of Ashford. The blockade gave way to the coastguard and as the century progressed and the duty changes made traditional smuggling less profitable, so the fishermen of Hythe turned their attention to other activities. Other human dangers were also decreasing although as late as 1803 Henry Mackeson was writing: 'The press gangs were active along the shore yesterday in taking men even from the fishing boats', a risk which continued until 1815.

Natural hazards at sea were at last being tackled. The great pioneer of lifeboats, Lionel Lukin, is buried in St Leonard's churchyard. His patent for such boats was taken out in 1785. He retired to Elm House, near the parish church, in 1824 and died there 10 years later. The first lifeboat station which included both Hythe and Folkestone was built at Seabrook in 1875, the R.N.L.I. being founded in 1824. The first lifeboat stationed there was No. 58 *Meyer de Rothschild*, which came into service in August 1876. It helped at the sinking of the *Grosser Kurfurst* in May 1878. In 1884 its successor, bearing the same name, took over and saved nearly 30 lives, one of the most dramatic incidents being the sinking of the *Benvenue* on 11 November 1891 when the lifeboat was launched three times in one day. At Coxswain Hennessy's suggestion, the station operated from Hythe from 1893, Folkestone having its own station by then. In 1936 a second Hythe station was built to take a larger lifeboat, the *Viscountess Wakefield*. A rescue service was maintained until 1974.

5. Lionel Lukin, lifeboat inventor. He lived from 1742 to 1832. The last 20 years of his life were spent in Hythe.

Another Hythe man, Sir Francis Pettit-Smith, invented the screw propeller for steamships, the first to use it being the S.S. *Archemedes* in 1839. Sir Francis was born in 1808 in a house on the corner of the High Street and Three Posts Lane. He died in 1874.

The 19th century also saw the development of the railway. Folkestone's first station was opened on 28 June 1843 on a line direct from London and was planned to link up with Dover. Hythe's geological location made a branch line unlikely; the 'Westenhanger and Hythe' station on the main line, opened in February 1844, seemed the best the town could hope for. With Sir Edward Watkin's arrival as chairman of the South Eastern Railway in 1866, some progress was made. The first sod for a branch line was dug by H.R.H. Prince Arthur of Connaught on 11 April 1872. It was formally opened by H.R.H. the Duke of Teck on 9 October 1874 to the cheers of the populace and a parade of over 1,000 children from Hythe, Saltwood, Sandgate, Cheriton, Lympne and Newington schools. The hope that the line would continue to Folkestone harbour was not to bear fruit. In the end, it was to close in December 1951.

Brian Hart has observed in his authoritative *The Hythe and Sandgate Railway*, '... Hythe ... prospered immeasurably [from] the arrival of the railway, despite the station being on the top of a steep hill on the outskirts'. There were three horse-bus businesses operating anyway, one by Henry Ovenden, proprietor of the *Swan Hotel*. The South East Railway opened their magnificent new *Seabrook Hotel* in July 1880, on a site formerly occupied by Martello tower Number 10. The initial confidence proved ill-founded; the hotel was losing money by 1900. A syndicate led by William Cobay took over in 1901, completely refurbishing the hotel and installing its own electricity generator. It was re-named *Hotel Imperial*. In 1946 it was re-sold to to W. J. Marston and Son of Fulham.

The year 1881 saw the Prince of Wales, later King Edward VII, open Hythe's new sea wall and marine parade, subsequently named 'Princes Parade'. The tramway used to carry building materials along the sea wall was left when the 'Parade' was completed, as it was felt that a more extended tramway would be created before long. However, it was not until 1 August 1892 that the Folkestone, Sandgate and Hythe Tramways Company was able to start a service between the bottom of Sandgate Hill and Red Lion Square, near where the tram shed housing the trams and horses was erected in 1894. The tramway finally closed in January 1922.

Elementary education in Hythe was vastly improved by the opening of a National School in the High Street opposite the *King's Head* in 1814, although there had been a charity school as early as 1729. S. J. Mackie, writing around 1880, notes that 'The National Schools (built in the 1850s) are situated in St Leonard's Place, and are very finely built of ragstone with Caen facings'. St Leonard's Place is now part of St Leonard's Road. By the turn of the century, Hythe boasted not only elementary schools for boys and girls but also, since 1896, a Roman Catholic elementary school plus the Ursuline Convent and, in Prospect Place, the fee-paying Hythe School for Boys and the Hythe School for Girls, as well as other private schools.

Hythe was developing the full services of a municipal borough. It still retained its Member of Parliament, although he was shared with Folkestone. Sir Edward Watkin was elected between 1874 and 1895. Sir Edward Sassoon and his son, Sir Philip, who lived at Port Lympne, also represented Hythe. The town had its own police station, staffed by a sergeant and five constables, and a voluntary fire brigade. Hythe and Sandgate Gas Company had been founded in 1851 and electricity was to arrive in 1902. The Hythe Institute, situated in Prospect Road, was built 1891-2 and endowed by Alfred Bull. It had a reading room, library, billiard room and a large hall on the first floor. Subscriptions were kept low – just four shillings a year in 1915 as opposed to the Bowls Club's ten shillings and sixpence, the Cricket

6. The first National School in Hythe, established in 1814.

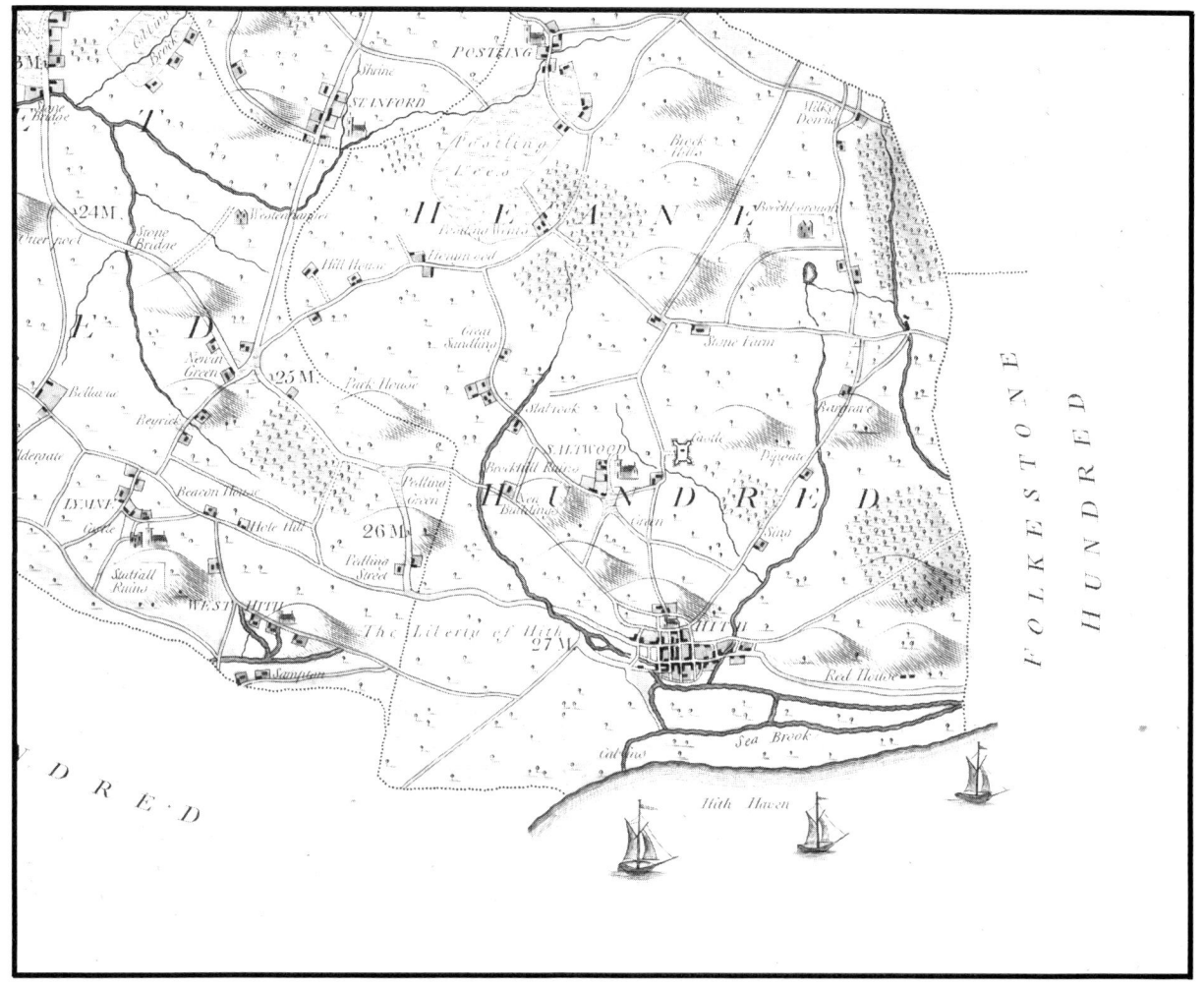

7. Hasted's map of the 'Liberty of Hith' and part of Heane Hundred. This map, which dates from 1799, is, according to John Boyle, almost entirely a copy of Andrews and Drury's *Atlas of Kent*, published in 1769, so that the research for it must have been done even earlier. John Boyle has also shown that Hasted's contribution was to insert, fairly efficiently, the boundaries of the Hundreds. This map shows the area covered by this book.

Club's guinea and the Golf Club's three guineas. The Institute survived into the 1960s when it was pulled down in order to help a road widening scheme. Nineteenth-century Hythe had a theatre and the advent of the 20th century brought the picture palace.

Dr. John Walton's national researches show that Hythe's appeal as a seaside resort from 1851 to 1914 remained fairly constant at about 50th in the top 100 most popular places. Its popularity was heightened by the development of Cricket Week to which Hythe Venetian Fête, a unique attraction in the country, was added in 1860.

The cancellation of Hythe Cricket Week was the first change brought about by the outbreak of the First World War. Others quickly followed. The tram service was cancelled, the horses requisitioned. Men volunteered or were called up. Over 1,000 went, of whom 154 were killed from a population of just 6,387 in 1911. Some of the 60,000

Belgian refugees that descended on Folkestone in the first weeks of the war were accommodated in Hythe. There was, too, the constant drive for funds, tens of thousands of pounds being raised; the influx of still more troops, especially Canadians, as elsewhere along the coast; the use of some Hythe boy scouts to assist the coastguards; the restriction of licensing hours and the occasional bombing casualties to be endured. Two Hythe men, Lieutenant Gordon Steele R.N. and Captain J. F. Vallentin, won Victoria Crosses.

Between the wars, fresh developments included the introduction of the Romney, Hythe and Dymchurch Light Railway by Captain Jack Howey in 1927, a public service and a major tourist attraction whose first passenger was H.R.H. the Duke of York, afterwards King George VI. Another improvement was the generous bequest by Dr. Randall Davis of his house, Oaklands, originally the site of a wheatstore, to the town provided that part of it was used as a local museum – the present local history room. The rest was converted into much needed municipal offices. The library, which was also initially housed at Oaklands, moved into its present premises in 1963. A former Lord Mayor of London, Lord Wakefield of Hythe, was also generous in his gifts to the town at this time – a lifeboat and lifeboat house, the rehanging of bells in the church, and contributions to numerous societies. This was acknowledged by Hythe when he was elected an honorary freeman and by a special Wakefield Day held in 1957.

The Venetian Fête, as part of Hythe Cricket Week, had returned with the end of the war. Hythe Cricket Club itself at one stage could boast as captain Percy Chapman, Captain of England 1926-30, a marvellous player with a delightful personality who became under-brewer at the Hythe brewery in 1923.

The outbreak of the Second World War in 1939 meant that yet again bombs would be dropped on Hythe, life would be rudely disrupted, men and women killed. However, since before the Conquest, Hythe had experienced similar situations and yet again the town would come through 'bloodied but unbowed'.

This book attempts to capture something of life in Hythe and the surrounding area from the dawn of photography in the mid-19th century up to the beginning of the Second World War. It is hoped that, as a result, interest will be kindled and further research encouraged so that even more is known than at present about bygone Hythe.

The Plates

Lympne

8. Lympne, *c*.1906. By 1910 the barns behind the bicyclist had been pulled down.

9. A rare photograph, taken about 1906, with the forge on the left and stores ahead.

10. Lympne High Street just after the First World War.

11. The interior of Lympne parish church in about 1920.

12. This photograph shows the Archbishop of Canterbury, Randall Davidson, and the Lord Warden of the Cinque Ports, Earl Beauchamp K.G., unveiling and dedicating the Shepway Cross in August 1923. This is to be found just outside Lympne on the site where, traditionally, the Lord Warden held his Court of Shepway. The Cross was given by the Earl and commemorates the deeds of the men of the Cinque Ports during the First World War.

13. Cinque Ports Flying Club, Lympne Airport, c.1934.

14. Port Lympne and its gardens where Sir Philip Sassoon, Hythe's M.P. for many years before, during and after the First World War and Private Secretary to the Prime Minister, often entertained David Lloyd George among other distinguished men. A keen gardener, Sir Philip was said to spend a small fortune each year selecting a series of coloured cigarette cases with which to demonstrate to his gardener the exact gradations of yellows, greens and blues he wished reproduced in the flower-beds.

Saltwood

15. Saltwood Castle before its restoration in 1882, when owned by the Deedes family.

16. The gatehouse of Saltwood Castle, *c.*1880, before restoration. It was originally a tower keep built by the disagreeable Sir Ranulf de Broc in the 12th century. It was turned into this imposing gatehouse by Archbishop Courtenay in the 1380s.

17. A rare if not unique early view of part of Saltwood village green, *c*.1892. The old Roman well is on the left, although the village hall and almshouses erected under Robert Thompson's trust deed of 1899 have still to be built on the right.

18. Another view of Saltwood village green, *c*.1892, to the immediate right of the previous photograph and from a slightly different position.

19. Saltwood green, *c*.1910, looking away from the Roman well.

20. Saltwood village green about 1909. At that time C. V. Hammon was proprietor of the *Castle Hotel*.

21. Saltwood church, *c*.1910. The earliest part dates from the first half of the 12th century. The eastern end of the chancel beyond the priest's door is 14th-century and the tower dates from about 1200. Originally, it had a gabled top, its present battlemented top being comparatively modern as is the porch. Note the small blocked window in the nave.

22. The interior of Saltwood church, taken near the beginning of this century. The Norman chancel was just to the east of the organ. The east window dates from 1330.

23. W. Clarke's Saltwood Stores, the mainstay of the village for some time, was opened just before the First World War and survived until well after the Second World War. This photograph shows what is believed to be one of their first vans.

24. The Post Office and Schools, Saltwood, c.1905.

25. J. E. Wood began as a fly proprietor at No. 2, Castle View Villas, Saltwood, at the end of the 19th century. His business built up and he started a dairy also, the two concerns being run from the Homestead, Saltwood Green, with the Model Dairy next door. This photograph was taken just before the First World War. After the war, the business continued as a dairy until the 1930s.

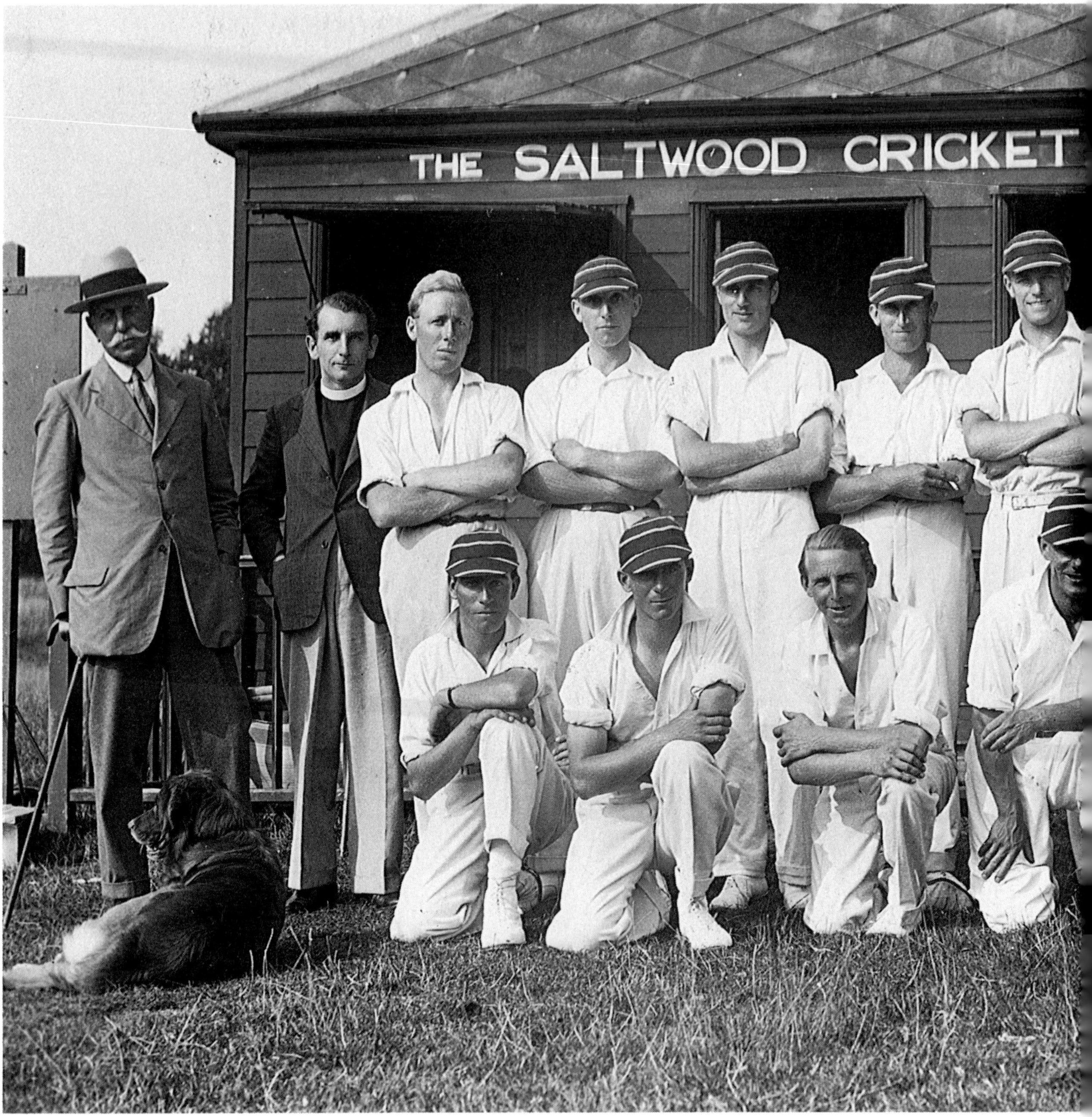
THE SALTWOOD CRICKET

26. Saltwood Cricket Club probably about the time of the Second World War.

27. The Saltwood model railway, originally begun by Frank Schab in 1924 and carried on by his son Alexander, who is seen here operating the train in about 1939.

Sandling

28. The old building, Sandling Park. William Deedes demolished the original house in 1789 and built the mansion seen here. The architect was J. Bonomi. The Deedes were friends of the Austen family and author Jane Austen was so impressed with the building that she used Bonomi's name in one of her novels. This square mansion with its 25 bedrooms was demolished by a 500-lb bomb in 1942. A new house was built on the same site in 1949-50.

29. Ashford Lodge, the Sandling Park gatehouse, Pedlindge, c.1907.

30. Some of the workmen who built the huts for **Kitchener's army** at Sandling, October 1914.

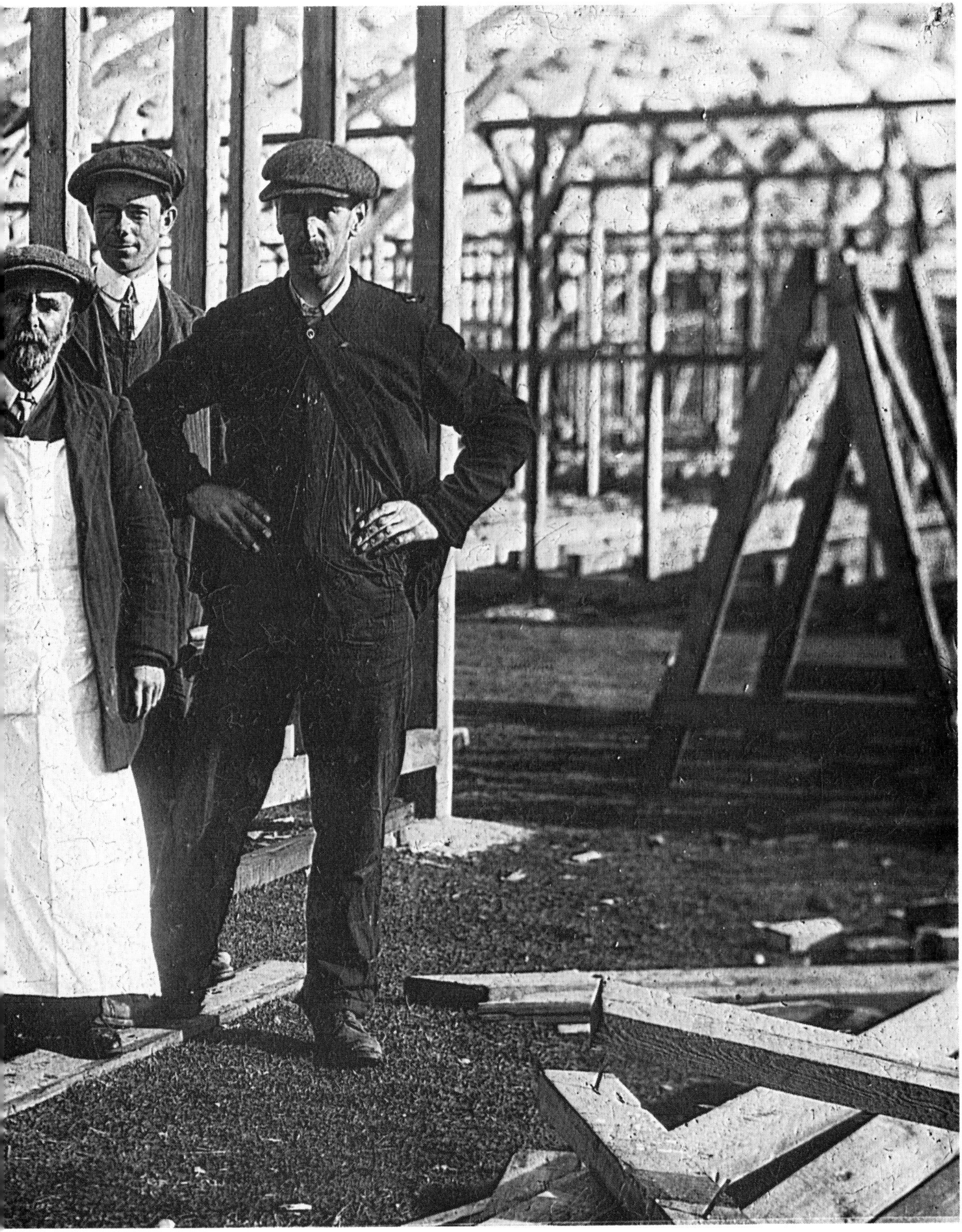

Pedlindge Church, Hythe

31. Pedlindge mission church which is attached to Saltwood parish church, soon after the turn of the century.

32. Sandling Station from an unusual angle, showing the new military camp on the hills. Note the steam traction engine. This picture is just pre-First World War.

33. A train prepares to leave Sandling Junction on its way to London. To the right, the platform of the Hythe and Sandgate branch line is visible. As the branch line became a single track in 1931 with the closure of the Sandgate in Seabrook Station, this photograph probably dates from the 1920s.

Seabrook

34. The *Plassey* washed up at Seabrook on 28 January 1883. This full-rigged ship of 1,680 tons, built in 1874, was sailing from Demerera on Christmas Day 1882 carrying 1,200 tons of sugar and rum. There was a crew of 50 with six passengers. It was caught in a squall off Dungeness. Two lives were lost and the ship itself broke up during a gale on 1 February 1883.

35. Horn Street as it used to be *c.*1910. The 'pub' sign can just be made out above the old man's head.

36. Horn Street, Seabrook, by the inn and mill stream, *c.*1920.

37. This photograph shows the old Horn Street mill of W. Martin Ltd., and was taken by local historian the late C. P. Davies in 1936. The mill and cottage have subsequently been demolished to make way for a small housing development.

38. Carts and waggons, the latter belonging to J. Jeal, the Seabrook building contractor, outside stables near Mill House at the bottom of Horn Street. The photograph was taken about 1900.

39. Storms surround the old Seabrook lifeboat station. Erected in 1875, the station cost £550. It later became a café and the building was demolished in 1956.

40. A view of Seabrook, c.1900, before the north side of the road was built on. Note the horse-bus in the middle of the road.

41. The view from Shorncliffe across Seabrook before 1920. In the foreground is Sandgate in Seabrook Station, the terminus of the South Eastern Railway's branch line down through Hythe. The line to this station operated from 1874 to 1931. The truncated line to Hythe was finally closed in 1951.

42. The main road from Hythe into Seabrook, in c.1910, before anything was built on the south side.

43. *Sea View Hotel*, Seabrook, in 1906 before any extensions were added. Robert Hinton had just taken over as proprietor from George Young that year.

44. *Fountain Hotel* and the view looking towards Folkestone from *Seabrook Hotel*, 1915. The landlord's name, James Tunbridge, can be clearly seen above a first-floor window. The brewers were A. Leney and Co. of Cheriton Road, Folkestone. On the right of the photograph can be seen William Wood Burkett's bakery, Seabrook Post Office run by John Blight and, on the extreme right, Alexander Knight's grocery.

45. A photograph of Seabrook Church of England School taken *c.*1905. The school opened in 1897. Mrs. Thomson, formerly Mrs. Jessie Pilcher, left money for the school. Her first husband built Seabrook Vale. She also bequeathed some money and land for All Souls' church, Cheriton.

46. A class at Seabrook Church of England School, 1931, which at that time was just for girls and infants.

47. The funeral of a former police sergeant, Fred Butler, in June 1924. He lived at 180 Seabrook Road, retired through ill health and died at the age of forty-six. A contingent of 20 men from the Kent police force attended. Some of them can be seen preparing to follow the last carriage while others accompany the horse-drawn hearse.

48. Mrs. Benton and Mrs. Skinner's Seabrook Children's operetta 'The Wishing Cap', performed in 1923. The children are outside Seabrook Mission Hall where Mr. and Mrs. E. L. Benton lived. Mrs. Skinner and her husband lived at the Seabrook end of Horn Street.

Mrs. Skinner's
a. "The Wishing Cap" 1923.

49. Army biplane 269 came down on the Parade on the Hythe side of Seabrook in July 1913. The pilot, Lieutenant Ashton, was unhurt and is seen on the left hand side of this photograph. His passenger also escaped injury, apart from a few scratches and a severe shaking.

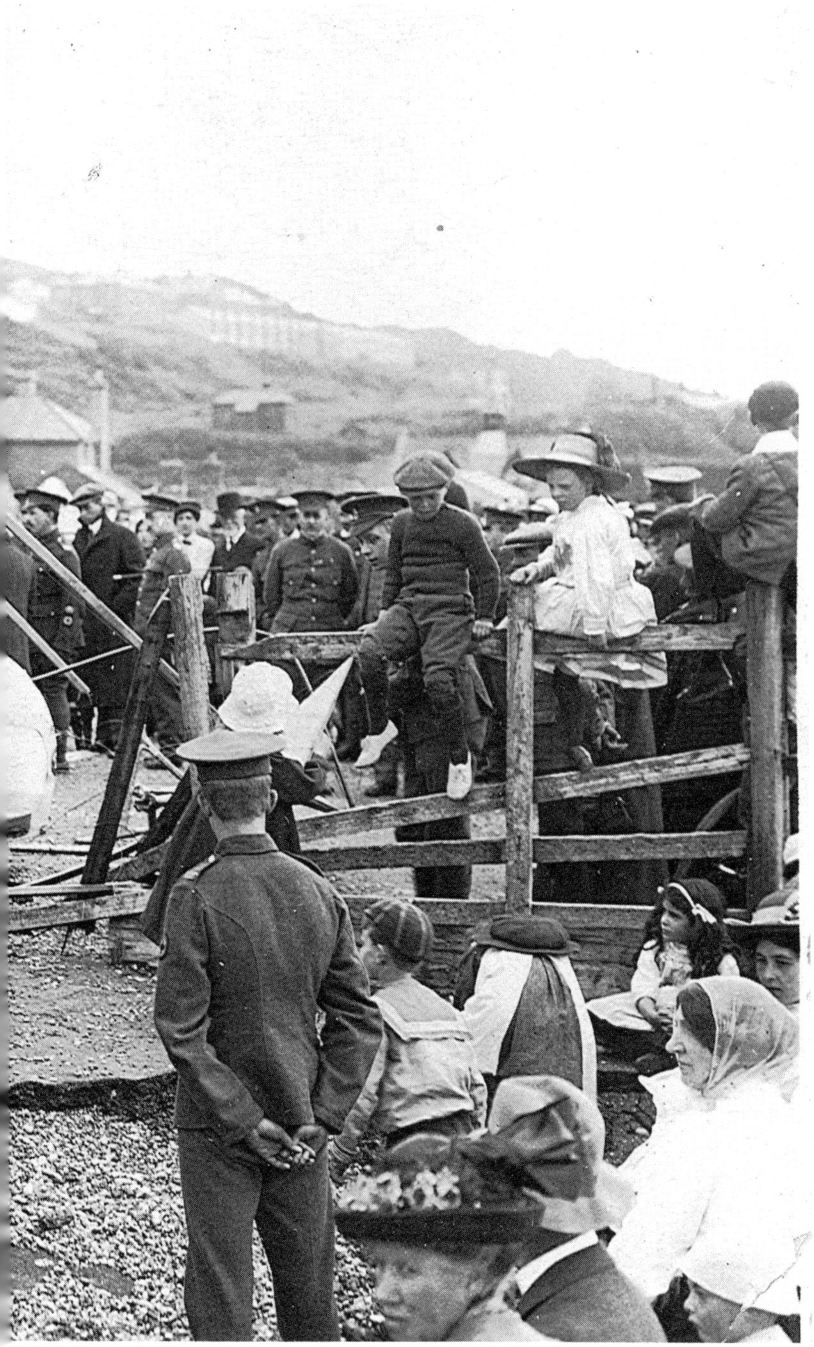

West Hythe

50. Studfall Farm, West Hythe, probably before the turn of the century and certainly no later than 1909.

51. The *Carpenter's Arms*, West Hythe, c.1905. This inn was certainly in existence by 1860.

52. Beating the Bounds at Hythe, 5 October 1910. The men in this photograph are crossing the Royal Military Canal at West Hythe.

Hythe

53. One of the earliest photographs of Hythe. The old bridge across the canal, shown in Westall's engraving of 1829, can be seen. The building to the right, partly underneath the trees, was used by military personnel. The original Methodist chapel can just be made out on the left, partly obscured by another tree. The photograph is thought to have been taken before 1860.

54. An unusual general view of Hythe, looking west in the first years of this century. Note the millhouse in the middle ground on the left, Dental Street behind it and, to the right, Station Road. Further back, the parish church can be clearly seen. Saltwood, on the top of the hill to the right, is still very separate from Hythe.

55. A general view of Hythe taken from above North Road at the beginning of the century. Although the sea front has a few villas and the *Seabrook Hotel*, about to become the *Hotel Imperial*, there is little building development in between.

Central Hythe

56. One of the oldest known photographs of the High Street, taken in 1872 by the friend of a soldier stationed at the School of Musketry. On the left is the original frontage to 'Propellor House' where Sir Francis Pettit-Smith was born in 1808.

57. A rather unusual photograph showing the dilapidated appearance of the east end of the High Street towards the end of the 19th century.

58. This photograph of the 'Smugglers' Retreat' was taken in 1892. It is said that the elevated loft was used by smugglers to light lanterns to indicate that the coast was clear to bring in contraband to store in cellars under this shop. It was a fish shop for many years, but was demolished in 1908.

59. Hythe High Street in 1899, looking east. Lovick's the stationers and printers are on the extreme right, while Isaac Ellis was 'mine host' at the *Rose and Crown* next door.

60. A very rare photograph of the west end of the High Street showing the full extent of the building known as the Malthouse.

61. (*above*) The High Street in the early years of this century, showing the Wilberforce Temperance Hotel and the Picture Palace. By 1927 the cinema had closed, to be replaced by a shopping arcade.

62. A rare photograph showing what was, in 1908, No. 18 High Street but which later became No. 40. Tooth-repairer James Gowers is publicising his services, and an advertisement for C. J. Newman offers traps for hire and a removal and carrier service. This notice in the window was to lead to the establishment of the large, well-known Hythe firm of today.

63. Fullager's fishmonger's and poulterer's. E. W. Fullager took over the management of what had been W. Griggs's business for many years probably just after the First World War and his business at 58 High Street continued until well after the Second World War.

64. (*above*) The diminutive 'Jumbo' Capon outside his bicycle shop at 100 High Street. The business had been combined with that of bootmaker at No. 47 but before the First World War he had established Capon Bros. Unfortunately, the business did not last very long.

65. (*right*) The Old Mill, Mill Lane, *c*.1908. There has been a mill on or near this site since Domesday Survey times. This particular mill dates from 1772 although additions at the back are Victorian. This photograph shows the top storey of the mill which some maintain was used as a smugglers' look-out point. The Burch family occupied it from 1832 for exactly a century.

66. An extremely rare photograph showing Mackeson's Hythe Brewery in 1909. It is viewed from the north, looking south towards the sea. The Mackeson family did not relinquish control until 1920. In 1929 it was bought by Whitbread's and ceased brewing in May 1968.

67. A section of the bottling plant in Mackeson's Hythe Brewery in 1909. The famous milk stout was just beginning to gain local popularity, having been first produced in 1907. Output continued to rise but it was not until the 1930s that Mackeson's milk stout achieved international as well as national sales.

68. Originally known as the Metropole Steam Laundry Company Ltd., the Metropole Laundry was situated next to the bridge on the one side and Pennypot on the other in Dymchurch Road. It did increasingly well up to the outbreak of World War Two but it closed soon after the war was over. This is how it looked around 1904 when Mr. Henry Wood was manager and the telephone number was 'Hythe 9'.

69. The view up Mount Street looking towards the High Street, *c.*1925.

70. Waggons belonging to Cloake Bros. whose stables and business premises were in Stade Street at the beginning of this century.

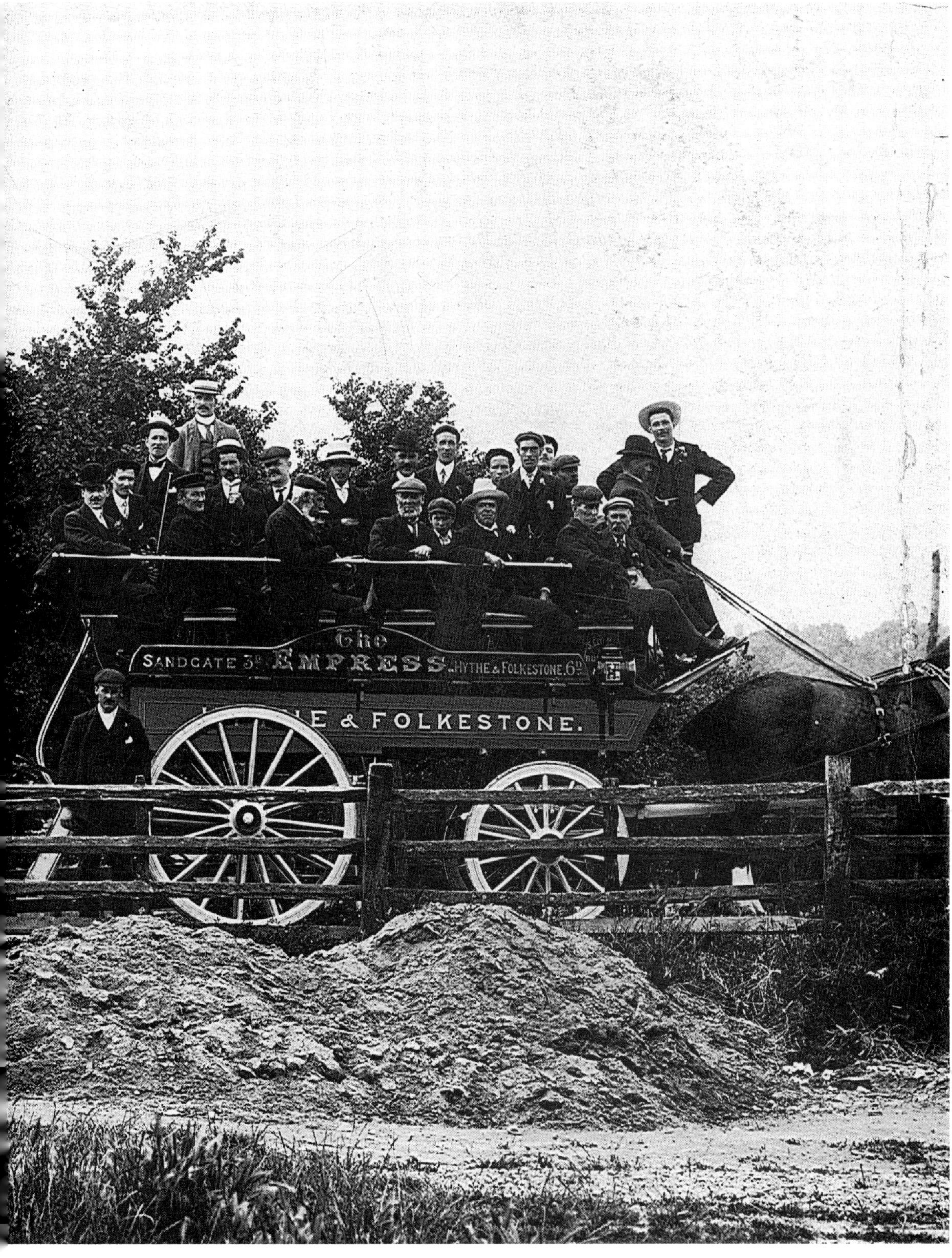
The
SANDGATE 3D EMPRESS HYTHE & FOLKESTONE 6D
& FOLKESTONE.

71. G. Swain's Albion Garage was set up about 1930 in Seabrook Road. Note the B.P. sign on the left.

72. Edward Uden, baker, grocer and confectioner at No. 7 Market Street where that street joins Frampton Road. This photograph was taken within a few months of the business opening in 1906-7, the premises being newly built. Edward Uden did not give up business until the end of the 1920s when he sold out to Peter Cooke and retired to London Road, West Hythe.

73. Morning in Red Lion Square before the First World War. It is nearly 11.30 a.m. and the horse tram or 'toast-rack' No. 5, which has just arrived, is slightly behind time as the journey to Sandgate is due to start on the half-hour. Behind, the tramshed and stables for the horses can clearly be seen.

74. An unusual view of Red Lion Square looking down the Dymchurch Road to the left and Military Road to the right. It was taken between the wars.

75. Troops entering Red Lion Square in 1915. Beyond can be seen covered tramcar No. 3 with, behind it, the tramshed. On the left, the other side of the trees, is Mackeson's Brewery.

Sacred & Secular Buildings

76. The interior of St Leonard's parish church c.1850. This remarkable and unique photograph shows the church before it had gas or electricity; before the current chancel choir stalls and even the present pulpit; still with the 'rented pews' crowding the chancel steps and, on the extreme left, evidence of balconies.

77. The famous collection of skulls and bones kept in the ambulatory at the parish church, taken about 1930. They are probably the remains of medieval residents of Hythe. They have been on display for many years. In 1816, Richard Chamberlain was given the 'privilege' of showing the bones, in addition to his salary of £5 per year.

78. The Roman Catholic church, Hythe, soon after it was built in 1893 at a cost of about £3,000. It was described as 'being in Seabrook Road', and dedicated to the Virgin Mother of Good Counsel. It replaced a temporary chapel in Park Road off Stade Street. Note the green fields behind!

79. The high altar of the Roman Catholic church at the turn of the century.

80. The original Wesleyan Methodist chapel, built virtually on the same site as the current chapel. Completed in 1845, it was photographed by Cobb in 1874. The present chapel was dedicated in 1898.

81. St Michael's mission church. This interior photograph, taken soon after it was built in 1893, shows the central window above the altar. Note the way the pews are set out.

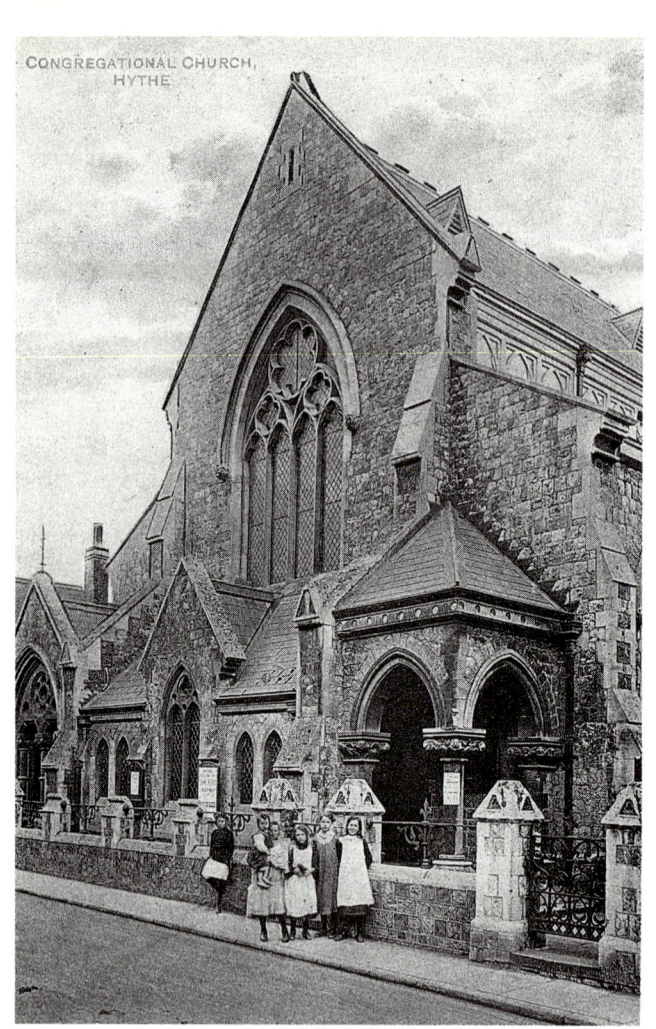

82. The Congregational church, High Street. It was built in 1868 and demolished in 1988, a new United Reformed church having been built in Seabrook Road.

83. A rare view of the parish church from the south with the Mackeson's house, the Dene, immediately in front. The Mackeson family first lived in the house in the 19th century. Members of this family included a Mayor of Hythe, an M.P., and the man who, with E. Osborne, paid for the organ in the church. The Mackesons finally left Hythe in 1959. The Dene has since been demolished and is now a small development of cottages and flats.

84. Hythe Institute, Prospect Road, built in 1891-2 at a cost of £3,500. It was endowed by Alfred Bull and provided reading, smoking and billiards rooms together with a hall on the upper floor which could hold 350 people. No smoking or alcohol were allowed in this hall except by special permission. Concerts and entertainments were occasionally given. It was demolished in the late 1960s to make room for a road widening scheme. The money provided as compensation by the government has been used to set up a charitable trust fund for local causes.

85. Mr. and Mrs. T. Elliott, proprietors of *The Swan*, outside their hotel in about 1905. They were there from at least the beginning of the century until *c.*1907 when another member of the family, George, took over for a brief period. During this time the hotel 'moved' from 131 to 59 High Street because of renumbering.

86. An unusual photograph of the 'toast-rack' passing the *Hotel Imperial*, c.1920. Mules had been used for a brief period but proved too unruly, so horses took over again. Soon after this photograph was taken the tramway closed.

Ladies Walk
& The Royal Military Canal

87. Ladies Walk as it appeared in 1870, looking from the south end towards the town.

88. Ladies Walk as it appeared in January 1877 when flooded by the sea.

89. A rare photograph of the original Ladies Walk Bridge which was swept away by the sea on 1 January 1877.

90. The second Ladies Walk Bridge, erected after the 1877 storm, which survived until *c.*1913.

91. In this interesting and unusual photograph, workmen from H. Dray are seen preparing timber for the new Ladies Walk Bridge in 1877 or 1878.

92. The Royal Military Canal at the beginning of the century.

93. C. Carter's boats were available for hire for many years on the Royal Military Canal at the beginning of this century.

By the Sea

94. While the donkeys make their way towards the beach, No. 5 car of the tramway turns from Stade Street into South Road.

95. The Promenade at Hythe, c.1900. On the far right near the sea are the changing huts for swimmers while, in the middle, the donkeys do not seem much in demand. The fishing boats are out and have left some of their rope ashore.

96. Looking towards Dungeness along the Promenade about the end of the last century.

97. These curiously oriental 'new' shelters were built some time before the First World War. They were demolished in the 1950s.

98. A group of Hythe coastguards photographed at the end of the last century. The coastguards, formed in 1831, were under the control of the Royal Navy. They had to guard the coast, keeping a look out for any craft that might be smuggling or in distress. They also manned the early lifeboats and managed rescues in their own galleys.

99. A view of the results of the storm of 22 March 1913, looking down the coast towards Dymchurch.

100. The *Three Brothers*, one of a fleet of colliers owned by Joseph Horton, unloading coal at the Stade, *c*.1900. These colliers plied between Hartlepool and Hythe, landing coal for the town at the Stade and at the gasworks beach. In winter, when Hythe beach was inaccessible, the coal was landed at Folkestone and transported by pony and cart to Hythe.

101. Seine fishing for mackerel at Hythe just before the turn of the century.

102. Fishermen shaking out herrings on Hythe beach after a catch, *c.*1912.

103. The crew of lifeboat No. 35 *Meyer de Rothschild* of Hythe, the second lifeboat to bear that name, being towed by horse through Sandgate after being launched three times on 11 November 1891 to go to the aid of the *Benvenue* of Glasgow (2,033 tons). Twenty-seven survivors were rescued although one lifeboatman, Coastguard Fagg, was drowned. At the extreme left of the boat, standing, is the man who was coxswain on all three occasions, Coastguard Laurence Hennessy, who received the Silver Medal of the R.N.L.I. as did second coxswain Albert Sadler. Hennessy was also awarded the Albert Medal. The only other crewman who was involved in all three launchings was Wright Griggs, standing third from left, who was awarded a Lloyd's Bronze Medal, as were Hennessy and Sadler.

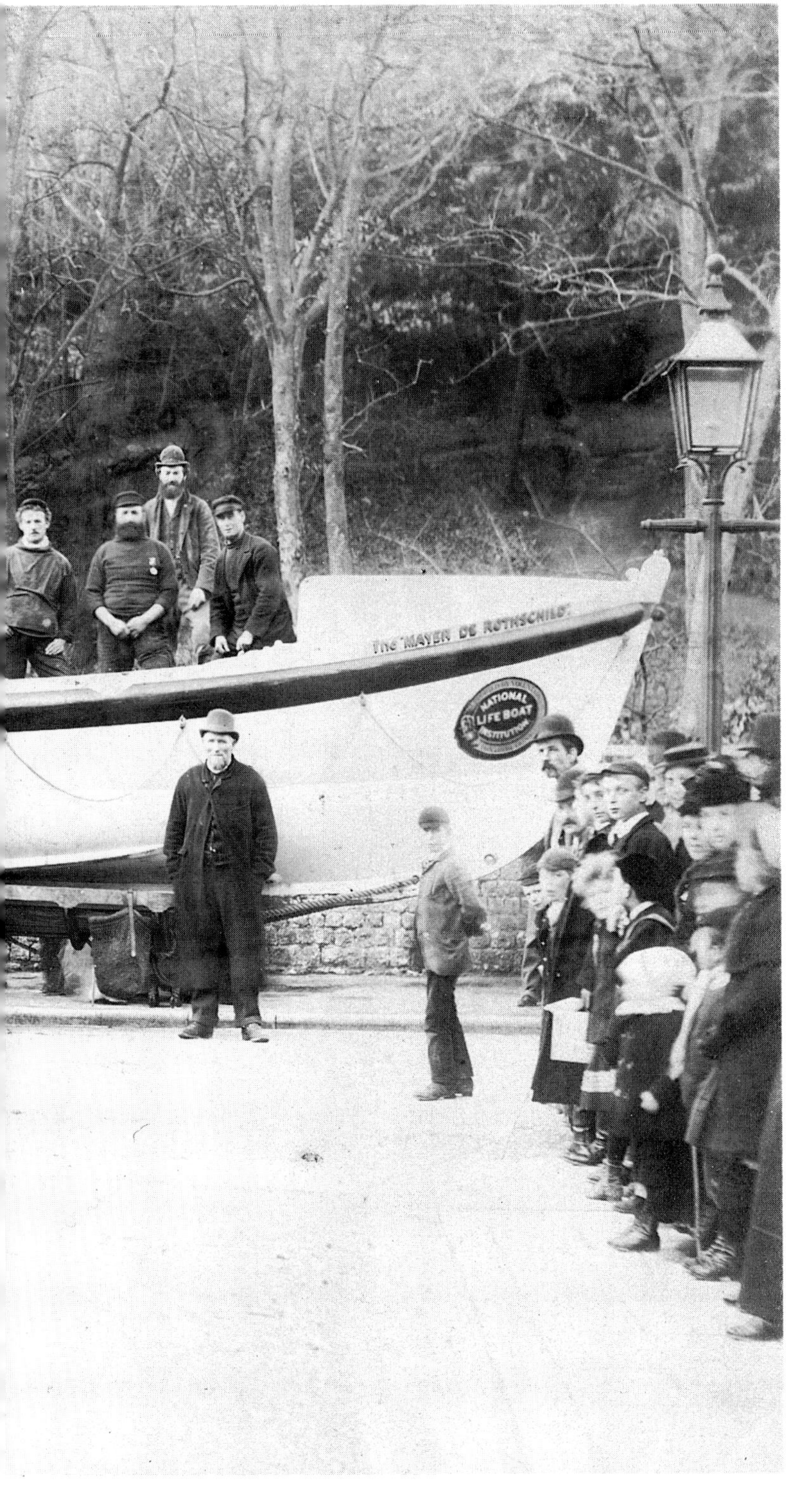
The 'MAYER DE ROTHSCHILD'
NATIONAL
LIFE BOAT
INSTITUTION

104. This photograph, taken about 1900, shows the old Seabrook lifeboat station. It was built in 1876 for £550 and was used until 1893 by which time Hythe and Folkestone both had their own lifeboat stations. This building was later sold and became a café. It was finally demolished in 1956. On the rising land behind can be seen part of Shorncliffe Camp.

105. Toby Griggs and his four sons, John, 'Son', 'Buller' and Dick, pictured in 1928. They were all lifeboatmen.

106. Hythe's second lifeboat, the self-righting No. 35 *Meyer de Rothschild*, originally based at Seabrook and given by Miss Hannah de Rothschild in memory of her father, Baron de Rothschild. This photograph was taken in 1907 during an inspection launch after Hythe had its own lifeboat station.

107. This photograph was taken in about 1934 of the original lifeboat house, Hythe. The lifeboat on the left is No. 610 *Meyer de Rothschild*, the third so named and Hythe's last to be powered by sail and oar. On the right is No. 726 *City of Nottingham*, presented by that town, which was the latest model at that time and engine-powered. *Standing left to right*: Alfred 'Winkle' Wonfor, 'Buller' Griggs, Mr. Niven (Hon. Secretary), Wright 'Son' Griggs, Bill 'Step' Cheal, Dick Griggs, Arthur 'Bung' Wheeler. *Kneeling*: Mark Cloake, Ben Cloake, Alban White, Mark Godden.

Railways

108. H.R.H. the Duke of York, later King George VI, with Captain J. E. P. Howey driving the *Green Goddess* on 5 August 1926. The Duke was the first official passenger on the Romney, Hythe and Dymchurch Light Railway. Behind them is chief mechanical engineer H. N. Gresley. The railway was finally opened to the public the following year.

109. Although this photograph was not taken at Hythe Station, it does show Mr. Hardy, first station-master of Hythe Station on the Romney, Hythe and Dymchurch Light Railway.

110. Hythe Station, *c.*1904. The railway staff, led by station-master William Fright, are on the 'up' platform, probably awaiting a train from Sandgate in Seabrook Station on its way to Sandling Junction.

111. A Southern Railway delivery horse and waggon under the care of District Inspector, Bobby Burn, at Hythe Station. Motor vehicles took over in 1933.

Glimpses of Bygone Hythe

112. This unique photograph, taken some time before 1877, shows the Lower and Stade Windmills. The mill in the foreground is the Lower Mill, said to have been built by Humphrey of Cranbrook *c.*1812-13. Eventually, it passed to Joseph Horton who noted in his diary in January 1858 that he had shut the Lower Mill. It is not known whether it worked again in Hythe. It was sold to Mr. Brissenden of Sandgate for £150 in 1875 and re-erected in Tile Kiln Lane, Cheriton, where it began work in 1877. The Stade Mill in the background was built between 1823 and 1832. It was demolished in April 1893. It also belonged to J. Horton whose house, 'Rockdene', was just to the north of the mill.

113. A Hythe windmill, Ruckinge. Almost certainly, this windmill was originally on a site in Hythe, just east of Cannongate Road and west of the old railway line. It is marked on local maps from about 1819 to around 1840. Subsequently, it was transferred by a Hythe barge on a final journey down the Royal Military Canal to a site close to the canal bank at Ruckinge, nine miles away.

114. Looking north towards Cold Harbour Farm. Sene Park, now a golf course, is at the back with Blackhouse Hill to the left. It is difficult to date this photograph but the clothes of the two men suggest it was towards the end of the last century.

115. Stade Street and South Road, Hythe, about the turn of the century.

THEATRE, HYTHE.

On WEDNESDAY EVENING, APRIL 19, 1809,

Their Majesties' Servants will act the COMEDY of THE

Soldier's Daughter.

Governor Heartall, Mr. OWEN.
Frank Heartall, Mr. TROTTER.
Old Malfort, Mr. HARDY. Young Malfort, Mr. MORELAND.
Captain Woodley, Mr. I. P. HARLEY.
Mr. Ferret, Mr. MOORE.
Timothy Quaint, Mr. LEWIS.
Simon, Mr. FITZWILLIAM.
Tom, Mr. SMITH. William, Master VINING.
The Widow Cheerly, Mrs. TROTTER.
Mrs. Malfort, Miss BARRY. Mrs. Fidget, Mrs. OWEN.
Susan, Miss BANFIELD.

END OF THE PLAY,

A COMIC SONG, by Mr. I. P. HARLEY.

After which, a favorite BALLET DANCE, called THE

APPLE STEALERS.

William, Mr. FITZWILLIAM. Old Squaretoes, Mr. OWEN.
Cuddy Softhead, Mr. I. P. HARLEY.

To which will be added, the MUSICAL FARCE of

Lock and Key.

Brummagem, Mr. OWEN.
Captain Cheerly, Mr. FITZWILLIAM. Captain Vain, Mr. MOORE.
Ralph, Mr. I. P. HARLEY.
Laura, Miss BANFIELD. Fanny, Miss BARRY.

Doors to be opened at SIX, and the Performance to commence at SEVEN o'Clock precisely.
BOXES, 3s.—PIT, 2s.—GALLERY, 1s.——Second-Price, to the Boxes, 2s. at NINE o'Clock.
TICKETS to be had of Mr. TROTTER, at the Theatre, of whom Places may be taken.

On Thursday Evening, the admired Comedy of 'The Heir-at-Law,' to which will be added, (by particular Desire, and positively the last Night of performing it,) the Grand Pantomime of 'Perouse,' or, 'The Desolate Island.'

Several Novelties are in active Preparation, and will be speedily produced.

W. Roden, Military and Commercial Printing-Office, Folkstone.

116. A rare example of a poster for Hythe Theatre after which the street is named.

117. The front of a programme of a musical and theatrical entertainment at the Hythe Institute during Cricket Week, August 1896. Apart from the musical stars, the second half consisted of a one-act farce, *Incompatibility of Temper* by William E. Suter, in which the three parts were taken by Mr. G. S. Wilks, Mrs. Perry and Miss Elfie Perry.

118. *Hotel Imperial, c.*1919, showing portering staff from the hotel together with its coach and horses. Alfred Swan, the coachman with whip in hand, spent most of his time doing the journey to and from Hythe Station.

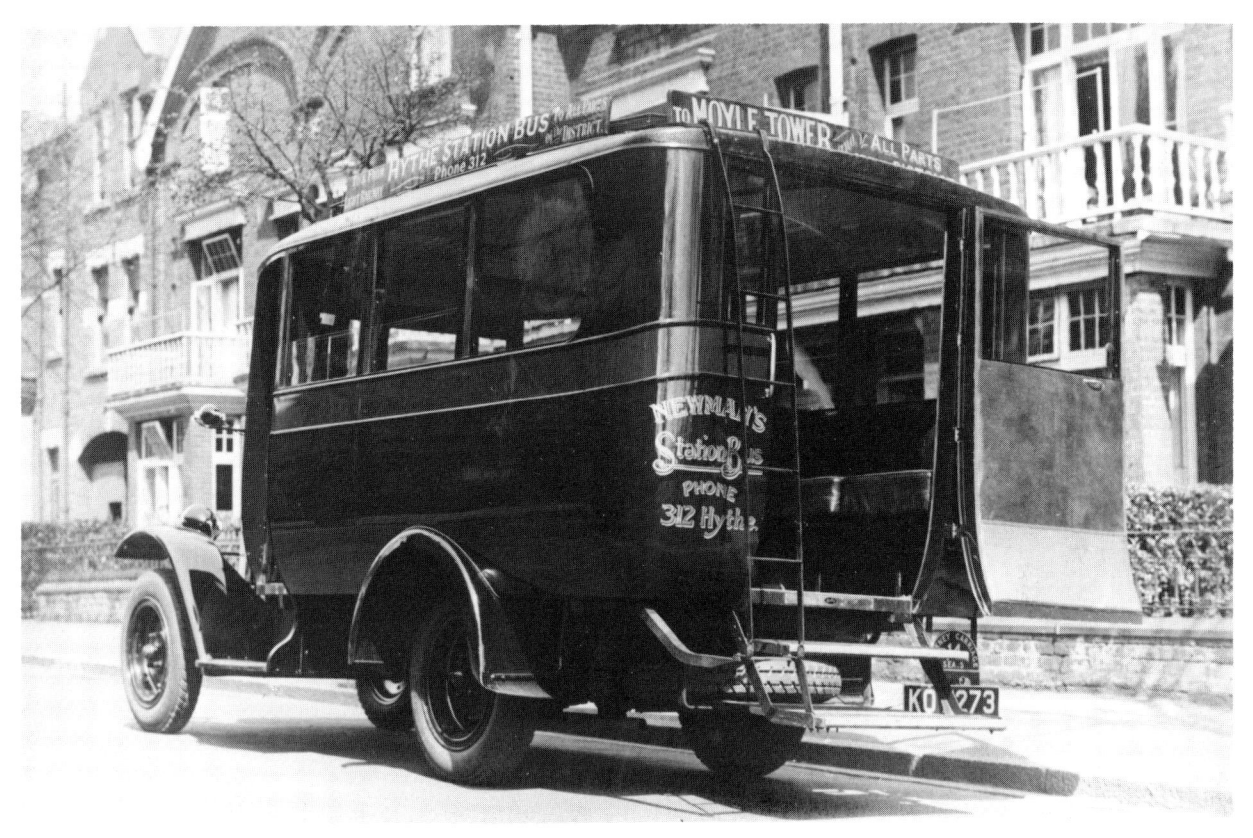

119. The remarkable station omnibus which belonged to Newman's, seen in Douglas Avenue in the 1930s.

120. Houses in South Road and Parade as they appeared early in January 1877 when the sea flooded the area. The Martello tower in the photograph is probably No. 10, the site of the *Hotel Imperial (Seabrook Hotel)* in 1880. The *East Kent Chronicle* reported that the sea rolled down the High Street, that people were rescued from the upstairs window of the *Hope Inn* and that water poured down Stade Street. Water covered the area from Hang Gallows bridge (the bridge by the Romney, Hythe and Dymchurch Light Railway Station) to 'Mr. Mackeson's Brewery'. At the other end of Hythe, the sluice gates at the mouth of the Royal Military Canal were broken by the force of the waves and water overflowed the canal, as can be seen from this photograph, for a distance of two miles.

121. Hythe Fire Brigade about 1900 outside the engine house in Portland Road. The entire force numbered 18 men including J. Ashdown, the Captain. Here, 16 men pose before the camera. It is believed that the Hythe Brigade was formed in 1802.

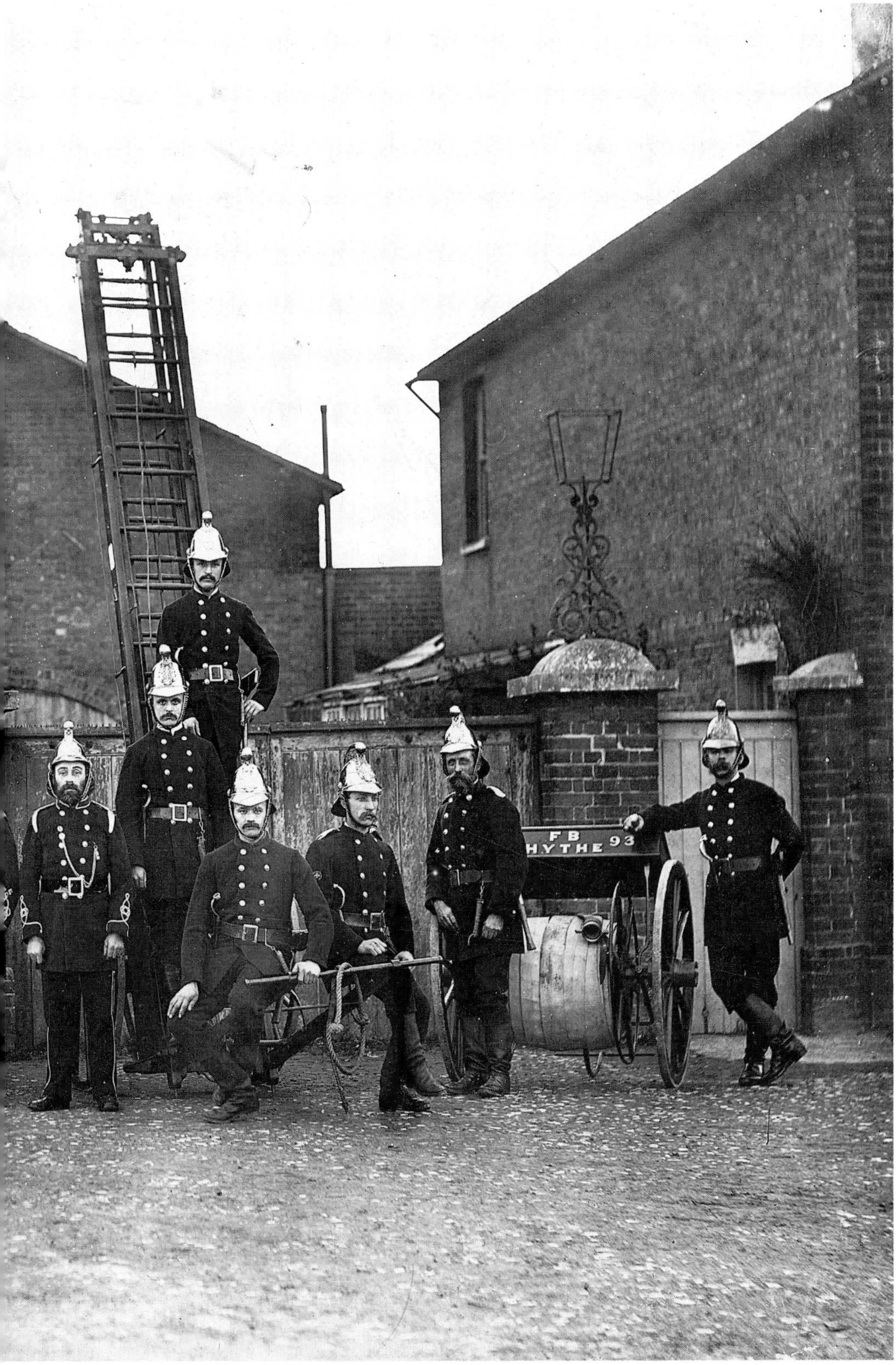
FB
HYTHE 93

122. The 'christening' of the new fire engine on the canal bank near Red Lion Square on 13 April 1905. It took Hythe's Mayoress, Mrs. T. Amos, four attempts before the bottle of champagne was broken on the 'Speedwell'. A trial run followed. Technically, it was a Shand-Mason 'Double Vertical', requiring a pair of horses to draw it. Alternatively, it could be drawn by hand. Three hundred gallons per minute projected a one inch jet 150 feet.

123. Burch's, millers and bakers of Mill Road, won first prize for their decorated waggon in a carnival, possibly that organised by the Red Cross on 16 September 1916.

124. The first known photograph of the Hythe Town Military Band, taken soon after they adopted the name in 1893. There had been a town band of sorts from at least 1870. Following various disagreements, the band split and in 1900 the Hythe Excelsior Band was founded. However, the quarrels were patched up and the two bands merged in April 1903. In this photograph, bandmaster John Nelson is to the immediate left of the bass drum with solo cornet player George Austin to the right. Bass drummer Harry Horton stands between them.

125. Hythe Town Excelsior Band photographed in about 1900 on Hythe Green.

126. The Hythe National Reserve Band just before their departure on a tour of Lille and Roubaix, in France, on Saturday 10 May 1913.

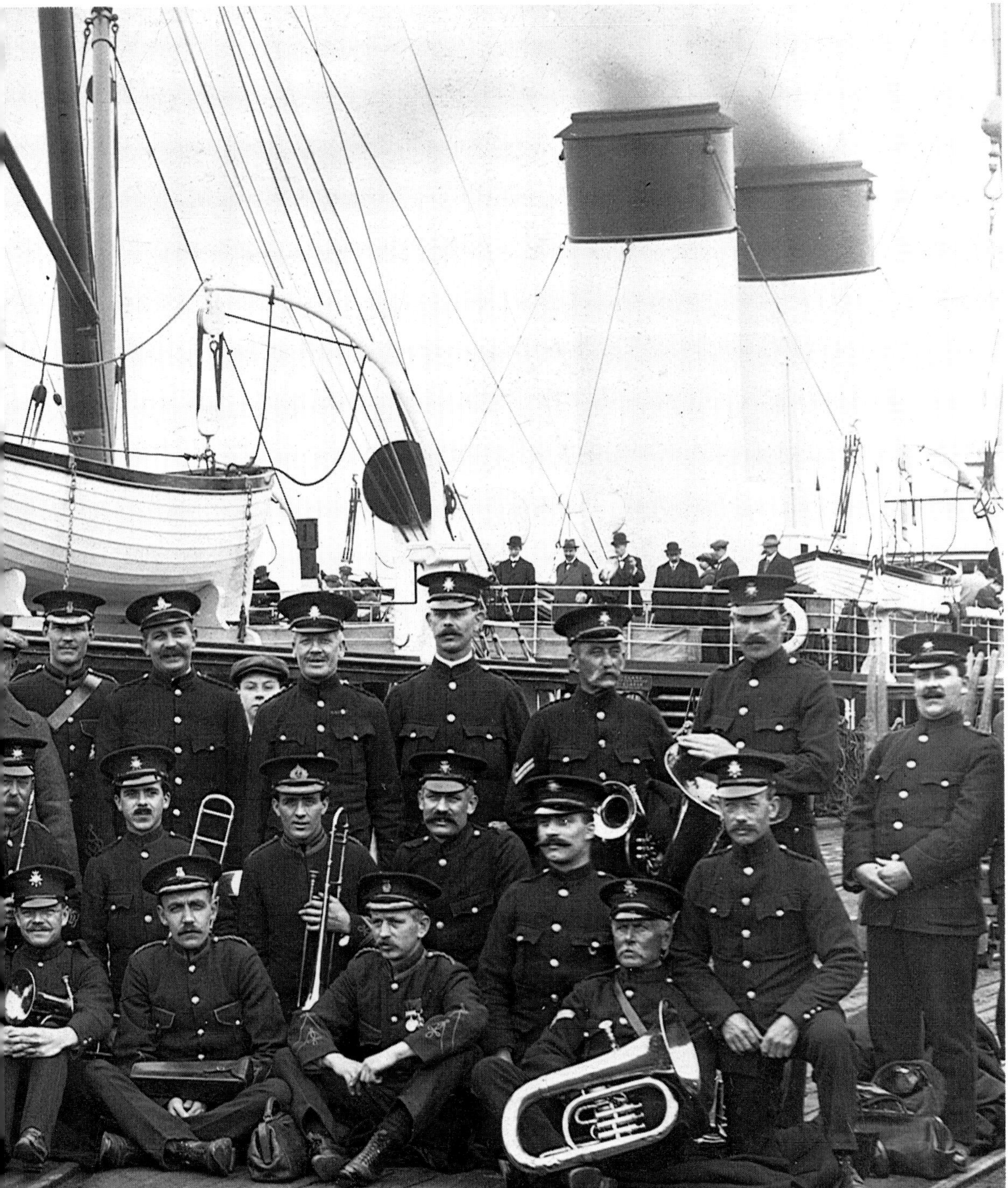

127. The proclamation of King George V at Hythe Town Hall on 14 May 1910 at midday by the Mayor and Speaker of the Cinque Ports, Councillor F. W. Butler. Schoolchildren, Boy Scouts, Territorials, the Fire Brigade and the Town Military Band as well as ordinary folk were all there. The Moot Horn was blown by Mr. J. H. C. Nelson; the Union Jack, which had been at half-mast since the death of Edward VII on 6 May 1910, was raised; the National Anthem was sung. Schoolchildren had the day off.

128. 'Titanic Sunday', 28 April 1912. A parade was loosely organised to collect money for the survivors of the *Titanic* disaster. It started at the *Hotel Imperial*, led by the Salvation Army Band. Hythe Town Military Band also played. Men of the Fire Brigade turned out as well as representatives of the Oddfellows, Forresters and Heart of Oak. They marched via Stade Street, where this photograph was taken, to the Town Hall where a hymn was sung. They collected as far out as Sandgate. Boy Scouts and others managed to amass a total of £48 18s. 10d.

129. An unusual photograph showing Hythe's G.P.O. staff in 1912. The man in the bowler hat may well be the postmaster, Mr. J. W. Wood. Post boxes were cleared six times a day and there were four deliveries every weekday! The stripes on the breast pockets denote length of service.

130. Participants of the Brotherhood and Guestling of the Cinque Ports emerging from the parish church on 11 June 1910 after a short service, led by the host delegation from Hythe. The banner is held aloft by a coastguard, while behind the Town Sergeant the badge of office of the Lord Warden, the Silver Oar, is carried. Behind it can be seen the Mayor of Hythe, Councillor F. W. Butler, talking to the Lord Warden, Lord Brassey.

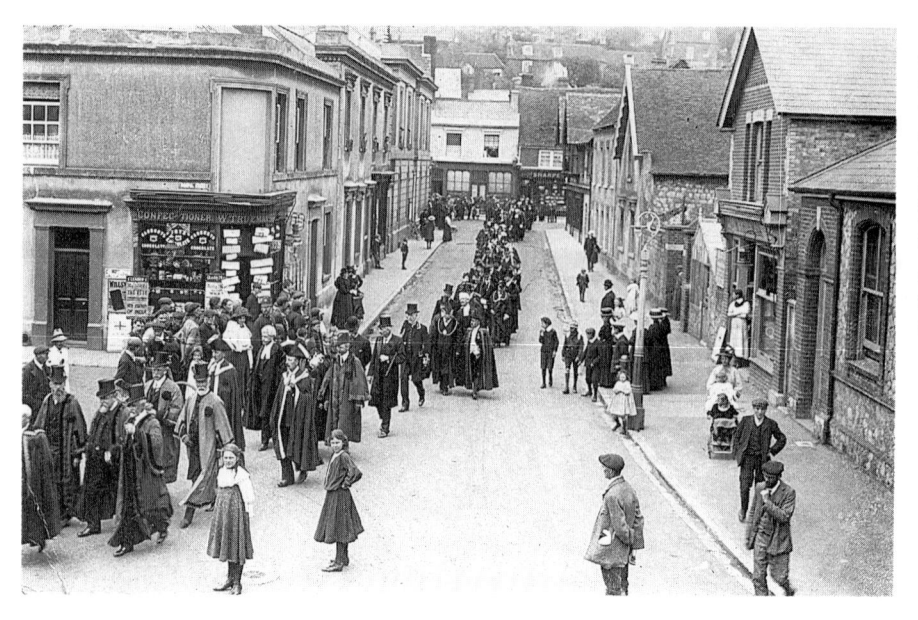

131. The procession of the Cinque Ports Mayors, dignitaries and attendants at the Brotherhood and Guestling at Hythe on 11 June 1910. The procession is walking down Bank Street from the High Street. On the left corner of Bank Street is William Trueman's tobacconist's and newsagent's shop. He had another shop on the opposite side of the road.

132. After a short service the men of the Brotherhood and Guestling went to the town hall for business, which included the coronation barons taking the oath of allegiance to the new sovereign, George V. A band led delegations of mayors, jurats and commoners from the five ports and two 'antient towns' to the *Hotel Imperial* for lunch, where this photograph was taken. To the right of the picture, six coronation barons in their court dress can be seen. The Mayor of Hythe, who was also Speaker of the Cinque Ports that year, was Councillor F. W. Butler, seen in the middle of the front row.

133. (*above left*) This rare photograph has caused a great deal of controversy. The Kent Volunteer Fencibles were almost certainly a First World War form of 'Home Guard'. The private's 'puttees' are none too expertly done and the significance of the black armband, apart from being a sign of mourning, is not clear. His rifle is a Lee Enfield with the sling tightened, as though on parade. There was only one 'householder' in Hythe in the directories for 1915 called Richard O'Gorman – the local Roman Catholic priest. Close examination shows the private apparently wearing a clerical collar and his cuffs, too, are noticeably white. Clergy in the army were usually given officer status and were not expected to bear arms, yet both these appear to be invalidated here. Perhaps there were few ranks because it was a 'volunteer' unit, and the rifle may have been purely for drill purposes. Otherwise there appears to be no logical explanation for this remarkable photograph.

134. (*above right*) The Rev. Richard O'Gorman O.S.A., Roman Catholic priest in Hythe for many years at the end of the last century and at the beginning of this, who wrote the biography *Hamo of Hythe*. Is he the Cinque Ports volunteer in puttees?

135. Paddock House Hospital, Hythe, 9 June 1917. Military patients in their distinctive 'uniforms' are recuperating from wounds and illness.

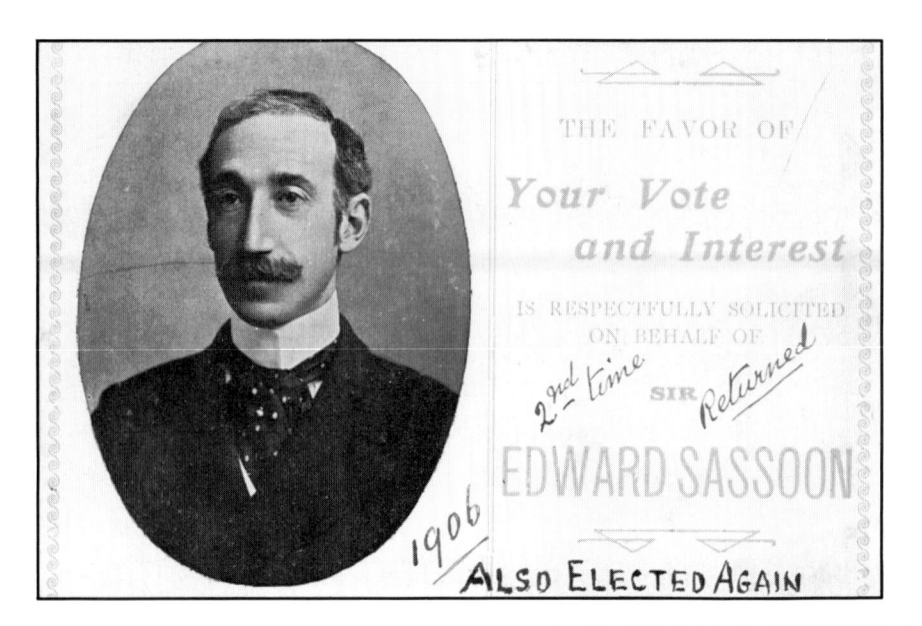

136. Sir Edward Sassoon was Hythe's M.P. from 1899 to 1912. He was descended from David Sassoon, born in 1792 in Baghdad, who through a series of adventures ended up as a moneylender in Bombay, India. The family did not reach London until the second half of the 19th century, and immediately set about making themselves part of 'the Establishment'.

137. Sir Edward Sassoon was first elected M.P. for Hythe, which included Sandgate and Folkestone, in 1899 when he won by 527 votes. He died in 1912 as the sitting M.P. and was succeeded by his son, Sir Philip Sassoon. These are some of the campaigners among the barrels in Mackeson's brewery yard, probably at the time of the 1906 election.

138. Sir Philip Sassoon M.P. standing on a tank, presenting it to Hythe on 11 July 1919. It was given by Sir William Tritton, a Hythe man, in his capacity as President of the War Tanks Association. It was accepted on behalf of the town by the Mayor, William Cobay, who is also on the tank.

139. Hythe War Memorial with First World tank and fieldgun in the 1920s. The unveiling ceremony was performed by Earl Beauchamp K.G., Lord Warden of the Cinque Ports, in July 1921.

140. The famous Venetian Fête began originally in August 1860 in order to provide additional entertainment during Cricket Week. It has continued to the present day, although there have been pauses during World Wars. Here is one entry from the 1938 fête.

The School of Musketry

141. A print of the School of Musketry at Hythe in 1860, seven years after it opened. The site is now occupied by the Seeboard buildings.

142. An engraving showing the rifle practice ground of the School of Musketry, no later than 1880.

Nº 836

First Class Certificate

This is to Certify that Captain & Adjt J. H. Nott of the Royal Tower Hamlets Militia underwent a course of training at the School of Musketry, Hythe and that he is perfectly qualified to instruct in the Theory and Practice of Musketry.

Given under my Hand and Seal at the School of Musketry, Hythe, the 9th day of Oct 1874

W. P. Ratcliffe Cn
Inspector General of Musketry.

143. A first class certificate in musketry which was presented to Captain and Adjutant J. H. Nott of the Royal Tower Hamlets Militia in 1874. It is signed by Colonel W. P. Ratcliffe C.B., who combined the rôles of Inspector-General of Musketry and Commandant of the School of Musketry, 1873-8.

144. Church parade setting off from the School of Musketry to march to Hythe parish church, c.1904. This occurred every Sunday and the parade was led by representatives of the senior regiments, followed by the junior regiments at the rear.

145. Officers' Mess, School of Musketry, c.1905. On the left is the chapel, the former lecture room. On the right hand side is the Officers' Mess, the Travers Library, the hospital and, at the end, the 'haunted quarter'. The entrance to the School was on the left.

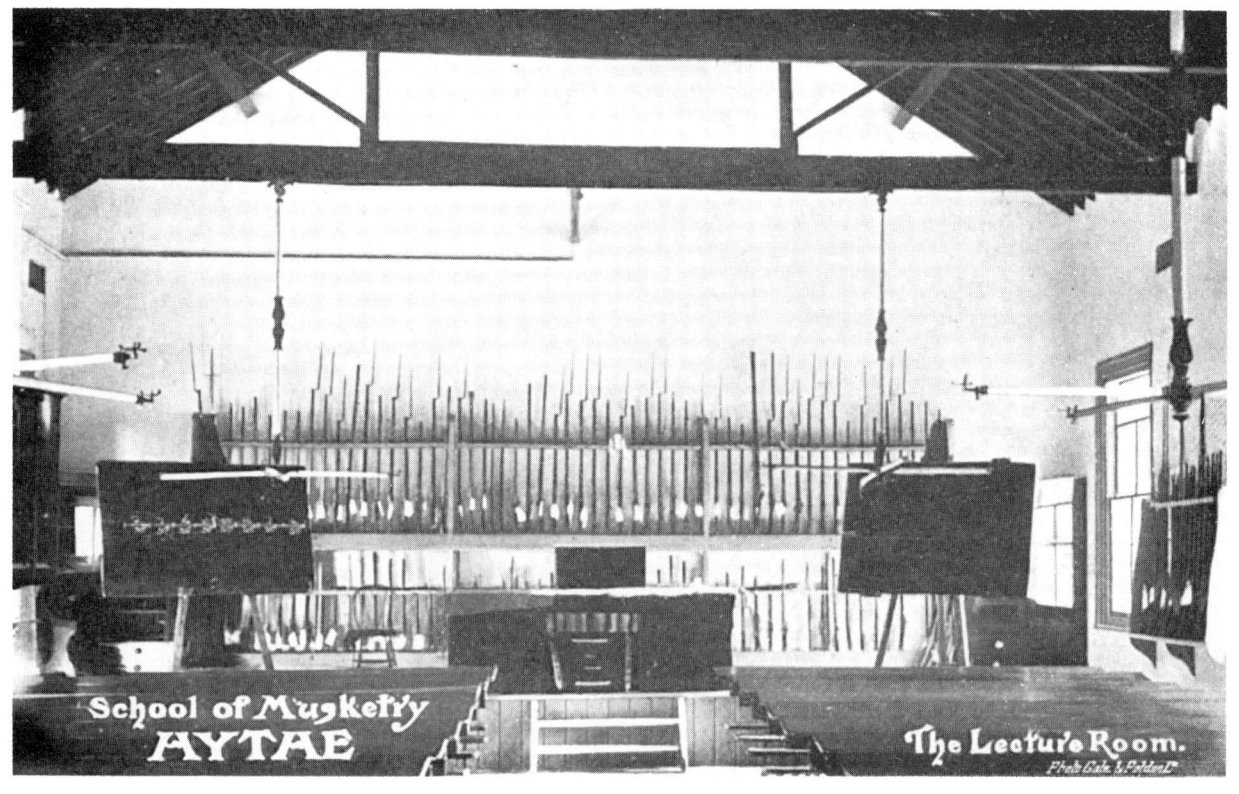

146. Lecture room at the School of Musketry, c.1905. This room was later turned into the chapel.

147. Rifle instruction class on Hythe green, c.1900. In this very 'staged' photograph, the group is under the direction of a Quartermaster-Sergeant Instructor who is standing. The rifle being used is an early Lee Enfield. Soldiers came from all over the Empire to the School and this group looks as though it includes a member of the King's African Rifles.

148. The cracked Martello tower as it appeared in January 1913. Until 1908 it was used as a target store on the Hythe ranges but it was discovered that the sea was gradually undermining the foundations. The tower was closed, marked as being dangerous, and later blown up.

149. Small Arms School shooting team, 1934. This was probably their most successful year and included two King's Medallists, the best shots in the army. They are seen outside the entrance to the Officers' Mess. *Back row from left to right*: Q.M.S.I. J. Horsley, Q.M.S.I. A. Austin, Q.M.S.I. J. Goddard, C.S.M.I. C. Miller, S.I. P. Ward, Q.M.S.I. T. Lamb, C.S.M.I. W. Rennie, S.I. J. Slowly, C.S.M.I. E. A. Jones, S.I. P. Walbridge, S.I. T. Moore, C.S.M.I. J. Collins M.M., C.S.M.I. A. Ellis; *seated from left to right*: E.S.M. C. W. Churcher, R.S.M. R. H. Amy, Col. H. Street D.S.O., A.D.C., Major D. S. Frazer, Capt. F. C. Papworth M.C. (Captain of team), Q.M.S.I. A. Southworth (coach).

Education and Recreation

150. Hythe National Schools, St Leonard's Place, *c.*1880.

151. A class from Hythe Junior School, *c.*1914.

152. Hythe Girls' School, Class I, 1914.

153. Hythe Girls' School (St Leonard's), Class I, c.1928.

154. (*above left*) Patrol leader C. Capon who was founder member of the 1st Hythe B.P. Scout Troop in 1908, shortly after the movement had been launched.

155. (*above right*) Cecil Oliver, one of a group of 'Coastwatching Scouts' who assisted the coastguards during the First World War, photographed in 1914.

156. One of the first scout leaders' courses was held at Hythe in the summer of 1913. It was visited by Baden-Powell, then Sir Robert, and this unique photograph shows him conferring with Scout leader Dennett of 1st Hythe Troop on the left, and Polish scoutmaster on the right. Sadly, the Hythe scoutmaster was subsequently killed in the First World War.

157. This photograph is thought to be the first showing the entire 1st Hythe Scout Troop and was almost certainly taken in 1909.

158. Bowling match, Boxing Day 1905. The players emerged from the new pavilion to play on the new green, not yet a season old. The pavilion was completed during 1905 by Scott Bros. of Prospect Place.

159. Mr. Ray Munds, who was groundsman at the cricket and bowls clubs before the First World War, is seen here on the cricket ground. The *Hythe Reporter* on 4 February 1905 said of the new bowling green: 'This is already finished and we have nothing but praise to say of it, and we congratulate Mr. Munds on making so good a job of it ...'

160. Winners of the 50 guinea Hythe Challenge Cup, 1910, outside the new pavilion.

161. A pre-First World War tennis tournament at the *Hotel Imperial*. The *Folkestone Herald* commented on 20 September 1913, 'The immense increase which has taken place in public interest in tennis – attributable largely, no doubt, to the recent Davis Cup Contests – is clearly reflected in the Hythe annual tennis tournament, which opened in the grounds of the *Hotel Imperial* on Monday ...'

162. Hythe Football Club's team for the 1910-11 season. This was the first season for the newly formed club. Their first match was in late October 1910 against the Worcestershire Regiment when they lost, 6-2.

163. Sunday League footballers from the 1910-11 season.

164. One of the earliest Hythe Cricket Club matches of which there are photographs. Hythe C.C. v M.C.C. was the highlight of Cricket Week in August 1905. G. L. Mackeson found evidence of Hythe Cricket Club as far back as 1855, in which year they played a match against the School of Musketry.

165. A. P. F. (Percy) Chapman, captain of Hythe, Kent and England. This remarkable cricketer, born in Reading in 1900, first played for Kent in May 1924 after he had come to live in Hythe and work as an underbrewer at Mackeson's brewery, which by then was owned by H. Simmonds. The same year he made his first appearance for England in this country against South Africa at Edgbaston, although he had already toured with an M.C.C. side 1922-3. In 1924 he played for Hythe on three occasions, scoring 129, 112 and 174, and made at least one appearance for the brewery cricket team. After his success as England captain in 1926, he received a telegram from the Prime Minister and a note from the King. It was while he was playing for Hythe on 13 August 1931 that he heard that he had been dropped by England. He scored 27 first class centuries between 1920 and 1938, three of them at Folkestone. He played for Kent between 1924 and 1938. He played in Test Matches 1924-31, scoring 925 runs in 36 innings. He played for Hythe 1923-31 and possibly later. He died in Alton, Hampshire, on 16 September 1961.

The End of an Era

166. The bomb damage from the incident of 4 October 1940, looking north from the High Street.

167. The bomb that fell on the arcade in the High Street on 4 October 1940: looking south after the initial clearing up.

168. One bomb dropped very close to St Leonard's parish church on 4 October 1940, blowing out the east window. The size of the crater can be gauged by the height of the rescue worker.

Bibliography

Articles
Cave-Brown, Rev. J., 'Knights of the Shire for Kent', *Archaeologia Cantiana, vol. XXI* (1895)
Clark, Kenneth M., 'The Cinque Ports Confederation', *Bygone Kent, vol. 7 No. 12* (December 1986)
Dulley, A. J. F., 'Four Kent Towns at the End of the Middle Ages', *Archaeologia Cantiana, vol. LXXXI* (1966)
Frampton, Rev. T. S., 'Vicars of St Mary West Hythe', *Archaeologia Cantiana, vol. XXX* (1914)
Hussey, Christopher, 'Sandling Park', *Country Life* (July 1954)
Jordan, Prof. W. K., 'Social Institutions in Kent 1480-1660', *Archaeologia Cantiana, vol. LXXV* (1961)
Jones, Dr. M. V., 'Election Issues and the Borough Elections in Mid 17th Century Kent', *Archaeologia Cantiana, vol. LXXXV* (1970)
Kett, John, 'Hythe's Ancient Hostelry', *Kent Life* (February 1983)
Mirams, Michael D., 'The Taverns and Alehouses of Hythe', *Bygone Kent vol. 18 No. 3* (March 1987)
Rutten, W. L., 'Sandgate Castle 1539-40', *Archaeologia Cantiana, vol. XX* (1893)
Scott-Robertson, Canon W. A., 'Medieval Folkestone', *Archaeologia Cantiana vol. X* (1875)
Scott-Robertson, Canon W. A., 'The Passion Play and Interludes at New Romney', *Archaeologia Cantiana, vol. XIII* (1880)
Statham, Rev. S. P. H., 'Dover Chamberlain's Accounts 1365-67', *Archaeologia Cantiana, vol. XXV* (1902)

Books
Abell, H. F., *History of Kent* (1898)
Boyle, John, *In Quest of Hasted* (1984)
Burrows, Prof. M., *Historic Towns: Cinque Ports* (1895)
Cobbett, William, *Rural Rides* (1830)
Dale, Rev. H. D., *The Ancient Town of Hythe and St Leonard's Church, Kent* (1931)
Douch, John, *Flogging Joey's Warriors* (1985)
Forbes, Duncan, *Hythe Haven* (1982)
Fraser, Antonia, (Ed.) *The Lives of the Kings and Queens of England* (1975)
Guy, John, *Kent Castles* (1980)
Hart, Brian, *The Hythe and Sandgate Railway* (1987)
Igglesden, Charles, *A Saunter Through Kent With Pen and Pencil, vol. XXIV* (1930)
Jessup, Frank W., *A History of Kent* (1974)
Jones, L. R., *Metropole, Folkestone: The Old ... The New* (1969)
Lambarde, William, *Perambulations of Kent* (1970 ed.)
Lemmon, David, *Percy Chapman, A Biography* (1985)
Mackie, S. J., *Folkestone and Its Neighbourhood* (1883)

Miller, G. Anderson, *Noble Martyrs of Kent* (c.1935)
Mothersole, Jessie, *The Saxon Shore* (1924)
Murray, W. J. C. *Romney Marsh* (3rd ed. 1982)
Rainbird, G. M., *Inns of Kent* (1949)
Walton, John, *The English Seaside Resort: A Social History 1750-1914* (1983)
Witney, K. P., *The Kingdom of Kent* (1982)

Directories
Kelly's Directory of Folkestone, Sandgate and Hythe (1927-39)
Kelly's Directory of Kent (1934)
Parson's Directory of Folkestone and District (1915 and 1925)
Pike's Folkestone, Hythe and Sandgate Directory (1901-11)

Local Guides and Monographs
Anon. *Lympne Castle, Kent*
Barker, Jack F., *The Saxon Origins of St Leonard's Church, Hythe* (1984)
Boreham, Brian, *Martello Towers* (1986)
Dale, Rev. H. D. and Villiers, Major O. G., *Saltwood Parish Church* (1962)
Davis, J. A., *The Roman Road from Lympne to Dover* (1979)
Martin, F. H., *Lionel Lukin, 18th Century Life-Boat Inventor* (1982)
Parsons, Capt. A. J., *A Brief History of the Small Arms School Corps and the Small Arms Wing, School of Infantry, Hythe* (1953)
Philp, Brian, *Romney Marsh and the Roman Fort at Lympne* (1982)
Pitts, Rev. H. A., *XIX Century Fragments of Methodist History of Hythe, Kent* (1969)
Pitts, Rev. H. A., *More XIX Century Fragments of Methodist History of Hythe, Kent* (1970)
Whitney, Charles E., *St Leonard's Church Historical Guide* (1976)

Miscellaneous
Anon, *The Mackeson Story* (1960)
Folkestone and Hythe Herald (Various editions 1895-1906)
Folkestone, Hythe, Sandgate and Cheriton Herald (Various editions 1906-35)
Hythe Town Military Band Centenary Concert Souvenir Programme (August 1980)
Morris, Dr. John R. (Ed.), *Domesday Book: Kent* (1983)
Whitney, Charles E., *The Spanish Armada 1588: Preparations to Oppose it in Folkestone, Hythe and the Surrounding Area* (un-published lecture, 1988)
Wrottesley, Capt., *A Report on the Royal Military Canal, Hythe* (March 1857)